PROTECTION DOGS
For You And Your Family

Edward Weiss, M.D.
Thomas G. Rose

Edited by
Mary Garland Jonas

Cover Design by
Bob Groves

Pen and ink drawings by
Lisa Ober

D1598317

DENLINGER'S PUBLISHERS, LTD.
Box 76, Fairfax, Virginia 22030

Library of Congress Cataloging-in-Publication Data

Weiss, Edward.
    Protection dogs for you and your family / by
Edward Weiss, Edward G. Rose: edited by Mary
Garland Jonas : cover design by Bob Groves : pen
and ink drawings by Lisa Ober.
        p. cm.
    ISBN 0-87714-151-7
    1. Watchdogs. I. Rose, Thomas G. II. Jonas,
Mary Garland.
    III. Title.
    SF428.8.W45 1992
    636.7'086—dc20
                                                91-31514

Dedication

To VOSS, BLANKA, SIMBA, and MAGIC

Doberman Pinscher, classic guard dog. His gaze is steady. He is ready for action.

Table of Contents

Pictured on the front cover of this book are (largest to smallest) Daniel, Byron, and Douglas Weiss. The dogs are, sitting, Rottweiler Ch. Liberty's A Chip Off The Ark, C.D.X., I.O.P. III, SchH III, FH. Owner trained and handled to all titles by Susan Borgen, Seventh Place International SchH III Championship for Rottweilers in West Germany 1990. German Shepherd Karlheim's Oscar, C.D.X., T.D., SchH III, FH. Owner trained and handled to all titles by Ann Dolan, First Place 1988 DVG Open Championship. Team Member WUSV Championship, West Germany 1988. Black Giant Schnauzer Falk's Country Life Magic, first SchH III of his breed in North America. All three dogs are American bred and owner trained.

On the back cover is a photograph of the authors, Thomas G. Rose (left) and Dr. Edward Weiss (right).

German Shepherd Blanka Von Der Herreneiche, SchHIII, FH, C.D.X.T., shown with her owner/trainer Holly Rose, wife of author Thomas G. Rose.

Introduction

Dogs are an important part of the American way of life. National surveys have shown that during the past thirty years, regardless of economic cycles dogs are found in one of every four American households. Unfortunately, the dog in America is almost never permitted to attain his full potential as a companion. Usually he is thrust into the passive role of an animated toy. Although the average pet dog may at one time have had the potential to protect his family, now he often has neither the ability nor training to do this. He lacks this ability because his temperament and attitude towards strangers is trusting, and his desire to protect is feeble to non-existent. He offers a friendly greeting, may bark when someone approaches the house, and may be the perfect pet for many dog owners. Or, he might extend a warm greeting to the Boston Strangler, Attila the Hun, or Jack the Ripper.

We need only look at the dog's heritage to realize how little is presently asked of him. The dog has served the shepherd, cattle drover, hunter, soldier, policeman, and as protector of the home. What then accounts for the loss of his protective and useful performance in our present day society? The transition from an essentially rural country to one of large urban centers has eliminated many of the dog's functions that helped the isolated rural family. The dog today is the victim of multiple homes, multiple owners, and fractured families. The pace of modern life has made him an animal in transit.

The dog in urban America faces the same stresses and changes that have affected traditional family life. Historically the dog's value to man has emphasized the animal's unfailing loyalty, stability and protectiveness. Though we as individuals still have need for the qualities the dog offers, modern life style makes our interaction with the dog difficult. We have become a disposable society in which mobility, change, and sequential homes have made owning a dog difficult. Then why do we persist in having dogs in our homes?

Life in urban America has become dangerous. Crime against people is all too frequent and the victims are usually the least likely to be able to defend themselves. The presence of crime makes us think back to the canine companion who, over the centuries, has guarded flocks, been a soldier, and protected the home. The difficulties of keeping a dog are often outweighed by the nonjudgemental companionship and the potential protection that he affords.

Within the last several years we learned of two outstanding cases of a dogs serving to protect their owners. The first case we knew of first-hand, as the lady involved was then a student at our dog training school. This lady was saved by her German Shepherd, Sarge, from a man who was choking her during an attempted robbery. In the early morning hours a man entered the all-night convenience store where she was working and asked to use the phone. He suddenly grabbed her, demanding money. When she resisted he began to choke her. Sarge, who was on a stay command in another part of the store, broke his command and ran to save her. Sarge grabbed the robber's arm and drew blood with his crushing bite. The felon immediately released her, struggled to free himself, and ran from the store leaving a trail of blood. We still have the opportunity to see Sarge when his owner brings him to training classes.

Within a year after the story of Sarge our local area was informed by the news media of a nurse who also was saved by her dog. The nurse returned to her townhouse after an exhausting ten hour night shift. She left her clothes strewn across the bedroom as she made her way to the shower. She was so tired that she barely greeted Muffin, her four-year old St. Bernard mix. The dog was pushed aside and left in the bedroom as the nurse went into the bathroom and stepped into her shower. As the shower began to drown out the sounds of the apartment and wash away the stresses of the day, the nurse thought she heard glass breaking. Within seconds she was filled with fear. She heard barking, scuffling, screams, and muffled explosions. For a moment she was too terrified to move, but Muffin's scream of pain, a sound which she had heard once before, when, as a puppy, Muffin had bitten through an electrical cord, made her run to Muffin. The patio door was broken. Nothing could be seen in the dim light. She stepped out onto the patio through the shattered glass doors and saw blood on the rough concrete surface. In a pile of leaves and grass was a mound of fur, the sight of which filled her with horror. Wrapped only in a towel she stooped over Muffin and wiped away the blood covering her head. Muffin had been shot, but her eyes blinked and she responded with moans to the touch of her mistress. The nurse heard squealing tires and saw a battered delivery truck pulling out of the driveway, one door still open.

Muffin did not die. This attempted assault was reconstructed by the police investigators and it was discovered that the intruder had staked

8

out the townhouse and knew in detail the nurse's routine. The assailant had sought to enter the house when the occupant was alone. Muffin, kept inside most of the day, was the unexpected factor which interrupted this crime.

Our experience with hundreds of dogs indicates that this was an unusual story. The vast majority of dogs may have barked at an intruder's presence but would not have offered physical resistance to the entry. Other dogs who have been raised as "child substitutes" in typical loving American homes may not even have barked, but instead would have perceived this intruder as just another guest entering the home in a slightly unusual manner. A loving pet might have jumped on the intruder, licked him, and solicited play as would be his normal greeting. A third possibility could have been that seeing an intruder breaking into the apartment, the dog would simply have retreated, perhaps barking, so as to be able to observe the intruder from a safe vantage point.

We all want a dog like Muffin who loves and protects us and yet is not a vicious dog toward us nor aggressive to everyone he meets. An aggressive dog is very dangerous and troublesome to own. A dog like Muffin will offer protection beyond that of a burglar alarm. The intruder will meet opposition. The ideal protector will identify the enemy, sound an alarm, and engage in combat if necessary. Possessing this kind of dog is not luck or chance, but the result of breeding and training.

Muffin was indeed a rare dog. Since she was a "mixed" breed we will never know what was in her genealogical "mix." But most protection dogs are the result of careful selection and training for their owner's needs.

In this book we will present the basis for puppy selection, raising and training the dog most likely to perform with equal portions of love for his owner and defense of home—as did Muffin.

For most of us, when we think of a dog that both loves and protects us, we project images of Lassie lying in front of the fireplace or Rin Tin Tin leaping from a second story window into the midst of a gang of bad guys. Perhaps we remember the dog of our childhood, whose memory, filtered through the years, is often glorified as are so many memories of our youth.

The practical matter of obtaining a protective dog, however, requires an insight into our own personal needs, desires, and personality, as well as understanding the basic drives and motivations of our canine friends. The dog is an ANIMAL and without training, behaves as one.

We know what we want. We would like our dog to know friend from foe, be immaculate in our home, loyal, happy, kind to children, and, if the occasion arises, be an implacable defender of our home. Only proper training of a stable dog will allow us to approach this ideal.

As a dog owner you must be aware of the potential for serious harm that any dog may represent when kept for protection. Most problems result not from dogs that are trained but from untrained animals chosen for size or the aggressive reputation of their breed. Many of the recent accounts of children being severely injured by "Pit Bulls" or other types of guard dogs typify the problem of purchasing a dog specifically for protection without putting forth the effort to understand canine behavior and to train the dog.

It is important for the new dog owner to learn that a good protection dog may be developed from their own pet, and they should avoid purchasing a "natural" protection dog. There is no such animal. Most accidents reflect the negligence and ignorance of the owner rather than any inherent characteristic of the breed.

Unfortunately you may think such a dog can be purchased from the friendly neighborhood guard dog vendor. Your hope is to have a super dog. Or, to save money, you may be tempted to locate an unmanageable, aggressive dog that someone else has had a problem with and wants to "dump." As the new owner you may believe you can rehabilitate the dog with love and understanding when what the dog desperately needs is training. You may expect this new "guard dog" to arrive at your home ready for adoption, ready for action, and ready to go to war! Before you do this, you should be aware that without training your next cash outlay may be at the nearest emergency room and/or courtroom.

An acquaintance of ours purchased two Rottweiler puppies, believing that if one is good two is better. He was not knowledgeable about dogs but he had heard that you cannot raise two dogs of the same sex so he purchased a brother and sister from the same litter. During the first year the puppies were in his home his three year old son had wonderful playmates. The man thought training would break their spirit, so except for housebreaking, hc allowed them to have the run of the house. They grew into beautiful, sturdy and active young animals.

He noticed that as their size increased they became rougher in play with his son, but he saw no potential problem. He had also noticed that the female was showing signs of coming in season for the first time. One day after work, the two dogs were rough-housing together when his three year old son walked near. The one hundred pound male seized the boy, biting him severely throughout his head and shoulders. Within seconds the female joined the attack and was tearing at the boy's legs. The panicked father waded into the melee and barely saved his son's life.

The boy's wounds were terrible. The shaken father is thankful that the attack occurred while he was at home. He knew that had he not been in the house the boy would have been killed. This child's near fatal tragedy could easily have been avoided had the father understood even **the basics of canine behavior.**

The last five years has seen a great deal of legislation proposed to protect the public from vicious dogs. The AKC has positioned itself into championing dog owners against this legislation. Indeed this is the reason that they have taken a formal stand against protective dog sports such as Schutzhund where a dog must pass tests in tracking, obedience, and protection. There is much speculation about the true motives and politics concerning this stance, but one thing is indisputable: **There is no evidence that has ever connected protective dog sports with risk or injury to the public. Nor has any data ever incriminated "trained Schutzhund dogs" as a public hazard.**

In this area of hidden agendas, media hype, and panicky legislative bodies the dog training community would benefit far more from widespread access to basic information rather than confrontation. We have reviewed a proposed piece of legislation (designated 394-C and submitted by New York assemblywoman Connelly and assemblyman Bragman) hailed by an organization known as "Responsible Dog Owners Association of New York" as a way to protect dog owners from breed-specific legislation. Herein lies an even worse threat; breed-specific legislation is being replaced by supposedly neutral legislation which affects anyone in the legitimate protective dog sports.

Subsection 14 includes:

"Training a dog for unprovoked attacks against human beings. No person shall train, torment, badger, bait, or use any dog for the purpose of causing or encouraging said dog to unprovoked attacks on human beings. A person found to be in violation of this subdivision

11

shall be guilty of a class E felony, and shall be punished by a fine of not more than $25,000.00, or by a period of imprisonment not to exceed four years, or by both such fine and imprisonment, provided, however that this prohibition shall not apply to the training of police work dogs..."

Clearly the premise of the above legislation is that training protective dogs threatens the public welfare, otherwise why would anyone seek to classify this training as a FELONY with fines and imprisonment?

This startling legislation provoked us to do a search of the National Institutes of Health library for information concerning the public health problem of dog bites. Our research was directed to the worst problem possible—FATAL dog bites. Data was studied from 1979 through 1988 and is included in *JAMA (Journal of the American Medical Association),* September 15, 1989 — Vol 262 #11. The information discloses that very few people in this decade of recording have been killed by dogs. The total number of dog bite related fatalities occurring in the United States between 1979 and 1988 is one hundred fifty-seven. The number of dog bite related fatalities in death rate per one hundred million population range from a low of one in the states of Missouri, Kansas, and Nebraska to a high of sixteen in California and seventeen in Texas. New York, the home state for this legislation, was five per one hundred million population. Try comparing this rate of fatality to the percentage of deaths from motor vehicles, firearms or industrial accidents. Other interesting comparisons can be made with bee stings, spider bites, or sharks.

The dog sport community needs to have a sense of proportion with regard to the simple number of fatal dog bites.

Of prime importance is classifying exactly which dogs are the perpetrators and exactly which humans become the victims of dog attacks, fatal or non-fatal. One hundred six deaths could be classified as to the breed-type responsible. Only three of these (2.8%) involved a police or guard dog! Twenty-nine deaths were attributed to stray dogs. The overwhelming majority of fatalities—seventy-four—(69%) involved THE FAMILY PET! Any objective evaluation of these figures should set off massive warning signals and put the dog-owning community on Red Alert. The numbers speak for themselves; **untrained dogs account for more than ninety-seven percent of FATAL dog bites.**

The **pet dog** is most likely to kill the baby in the family; not a burglar, not the next door neighbor, and not the agitator (criminal impersonator) in a Schutzhund trial. Of those killed by dog bites, seventy percent were children less than ten years of age. Most disturbing was the fact that infants less than one year sustained 68.3 deaths in comparison to the overall population which was 6.7 fatalities per hundred million population. A child of one month or less is more likely to be killed by a dog than all other age groups.

Circumstance of dogs killing children older than one year have been defined in this study in fifty of fifty-three cases. Thirty-six percent of the attacks were caused by the child entering an unauthorized area, such as a fenced yard. Twenty-eight percent of the attacks occurred when a child wandered too close to a chained dog. The final piece of information regarding the circumstances of fatal dog bites involving children is the fact that forty-three percent occurred on the victims property. The untrained pet dog was the perpetrator!

The circumstances listed in the study of stray dogs killing humans included packs of animals comprised of four to fourteen strays. Over sixty-four percent of deaths from strays involved two or more animals. We cannot cite one instance of a trained guard dog, police dog, or Schutzhund sport dog being implicated in the activities of a stray dog pack.

In the last decade forty-two percent of dog bite related deaths were caused by dogs described as "Pit Bulls." However, this information is misleading. The Pit Bull is not a breed registered by the American Kennel Club. The public perceives the Pit Bull as any stocky dog with a big head. Most uninformed observers wrongly identify Rottweilers, Boxers, Bull Dogs, Mastiffs, etc. as "Pit Bulls." The "Pit Bull" alarm is, in part, a reflection of media distortion. In 1979 twenty percent of the fatalities were attributed to Pit Bulls. In 1988 the media-fostered "Pit Bull" scare increased this number to sixty-two percent. The authors of the article in JAMA correctly recognize that breeds often may be classified erroneously by the news story. The article cites references from news stories that "any short haired stocky dog may be called a Pit Bull." They conclude that, despite potential bias, the type of dog that fits this description is responsible for forty-two percent of all fatalities and this type animal does not make up forty-two percent of the dog population of the United States.

The second most common breed found to be involved in dog related fatalities is the German Shepherd Dog. Since 1968 the total number of fatalities attributed to this breed was nine.

YOUR CHOICE

The Siberian Husky is charged with seven fatalities since 1968 and the Alaskan Malamute with six. Despite the comparatively small numbers of these two Arctic breeds, together they exceed the totals for fatalities attributed to the German Shepherd Dog.

Although dog attacks rarely result in fatalities, there is reason for the public to be concerned. More than two million persons are bitten yearly and more than one third of these are injured severely enough to lose time from school or work. We know of no studies that have attempted to correlate the percent of total injuries with the type of dog responsible. We suspect that the minuscule percentage of police or guard dogs represented in the fatal dog bite study would continue to hold true for all reported dog bites in general.

The concerned and responsible dog-owning community must make it known to the general public that it is the untrained dog that kills people—NOT THE TRAINED DOG! A dog that has trained for *and is competing in dog sports* has never been implicated in a fatal attack.

The general public cannot be protected against dog bites by ill conceived, misdirected, ignorant, and politically motivated stands by national kennel clubs or legislative bodies. Data and knowledge presented to the general dog-owning public should focus on the fact that the dog most likely to kill a member of the family is the family dog and the person most likely to be killed is the family child.

The present position of the American Kennel Club and some breed clubs in censuring guard dog and Schutzhund training programs must be attributed either to ignorance (for which neither group can be excused) or worse, to expedient politics.

Dog training requires a huge investment of time, effort, and commitment. Owning a dog mandates that the dog be loved, trained and cared for in a fashion deserved by this valuable creature. Anything less than the determination to fulfil these responsibilities is unacceptable.

Essential to safety is some basic knowledge of canine temperament plus adequate and prompt provision for training of any dog who is to live in your home. Intelligent and informed plans for animal selection and training are "a must" before you purchase a pet for **protection. Uninformed or impulse purchase of a protection dog can lead to the hospital or courtroom. Canine disasters are avoided when owners understand that a loving protector must be a "trained" loving protector. We will describe the education, effort and understanding required to attain this goal.**

This book is devoted to these principles.

GREAT PYRENEES

Definitions of Protection

Becoming the owner and companion of a protective dog is a serious undertaking. Like many things in life that are truly worthwhile, the value of your pet is dependent upon the effort and commitment you are willing to make in his selection, purchase and training. As a prospective owner, you should examine your motives, fears and hopes. A dog that will live with you and be capable of protecting you is a thinking, sensitive animal whose sensory powers, strength and agility often exceed yours.

Some compare a protective dog to keeping a loaded gun in the house, but this is a misstatement. In our experience of training and placing protection dogs, we have found they can be successfully integrated into households with children and elderly people. This success, however, has always been dependent upon the maturity and calm rationality of the owner.

Fear, unfortunately is an increasingly common emotion in urban, suburban, and even rural America. For those isolated, or elderly, a nonhuman protector is often a necessity rather than a luxury. The dog owner must be realistic and be informed as to the dog's strengths and weaknesses and how they are influenced by the owner's attitude and demeanor. A person with exaggerated fear of strangers, strange sounds or sights, and who is inclined to be reclusive, will develop a similarly unbalanced and neurotic dog.

One who 'shows off' a menacing dog is himself, displaying another manifestation of fear. This "macho" behavior, often masks an insecure person who signals to the dog his approval of aggressive behavior—sometimes without realizing it. Mr. Macho encourages his dog to 'say' the things he is afraid to say. An example of this is when the owner holds his dog's collar, pets and talks to him while the dog is barking and growling at a stranger. The owner disguises his satisfaction by saying such things to the dog as, "It's OK. He's a friend," or "Be nice. He is invited." In this example the owner is rewarding the dog's behavior by petting thus causing the dog to continue acting aggressively and frightening the visitor.

An owner who has purchased a protective dog may seek a situation in which to test him. Whether he is testing or showing off his tough dog, he takes private joy in the fear and worry this dog causes neighbors and acquaintances. This insecure person is using his dog to express what he is too timid or too inhibited to demonstrate himself. The dog has become his strong, dominant, confident, and aggressive alter ego.

A protective dog will behave with restraint and control if he has been brought up to do so. Thus, beginning with puppies from the same litter, your canine protector and companion will reflect the careful socialization, progressive and flexible discipline, and respect that has been his upbringing. Similarly, the canine "thug," property destroyer, and bringer of litigation, also graphically reflects his upbringing. Insecure, fearful or hostile people often mold dogs into their own likeness. The protective dog is dependent for his ongoing character development on interaction with his owner, and it is this interaction as much as the dog's genetic potential that will make him suitable for your home.

In the United States, there presently appears to be an epidemic of young children being mauled, maimed, and even killed by dogs. This has created in many communities the beginning of legislation to license, or even ban, certain breeds of dogs. The most publicized breeds being banned are the "fighting breeds." In many cases simply the words "Bull," "Pit," or even Terrier in combination will lead to consideration of banning these breeds. This public response is understandable. We do not need laws that will ban innocent breeds such as the small Bull Terrier, and ignore the danger that any giant or large breed like the German Shepherd, Akita, or St. Bernard pose. It is not the breed of dog that constitutes the threat, but the dog's owner and his negligence. It is not the breed or size of dog but lack of training and supervision that causes injury.

I have seen a child being treated in the hospital whose ear was torn off and whose face was disfigured after going into a neighbor's backyard. The dog that did this would frequently bark and act aggressively toward anyone who approached his yard. This dog was never permitted to live in the house nor was he ever given even basic obedience training. The owners philosophy was that he let his dog "be a dog" and allowed his natural protective instincts to guard his home. In fact he considered himself somewhat of an expert. He often said, "I have had dogs all my life."

When the young child wandered through a half open gate into the yard, the dog ran up barking at the child. The dog then chased the running child nipping at his heels and pulling on his clothing. The owner ran down the steps from his porch into the yard shouting at the dog. The dog ignored him and became increasingly more excited with his owner's screams and shouts. The child tripped and fell to the ground and the dog began biting him seriously. The owner beat the dog, which only increased the dog's fury. He was finally able physically to pull the boy away from the dog and the dog ran from the yard. Several hours later the dog was found by the police in a park. When they approached him he began to bark and retreat. They shot the dog dead as he tried to run away.

This tragedy illustrates the fundamental problem of trying to obtain protection without effort and understanding. The absolute lack of perception of what motivates dogs, and causes them to act aggressively is underlined by this tragic incident. And it was an incident *rather than an accident*, since the dog had responded in a predictable way. Basically one can see any number of ways that common sense, dog training, and sensitivity to what is safe, would have prevented this child's injury.

First of all despite having 'had dogs all of his life,' this owner, in effect, understood nothing about them. He shouted commands that he had never before taken time to teach the dog! What the dog heard was the intensity of his owners voice filled with excitement and enthusiasm. To the dog the shouting was no different than the baying of other pack members joining in the kill. The owner's shouts of, "Stop it," "Get away," "Don't bite him," "Leave him alone," were commands as unfamiliar to the dog, as shouts in a foreign language would be to you. What the dog heard was "LETS GET HIM!"

Initially, the dog did not attempt to attack the child, but began to chase him as a game. As we will see later, this Prey Chasing *is inherent in all carnivores*. It is no different from a puppy chasing a butterfly or a kitten a ball of yarn. The nipping at the heels and clothing was the ritualistic chasing mode of all dogs. The chase was intensified as the child ran and fell. The child's flailing arms and legs registered in the natural instinctual response of the dog. The prey (child) was caught. The dog had been raised as a tamed wild animal living in his territory, the back yard, with only his natural instincts to guide him. For the first time the owner who for months had ignored the dog was now suddenly trying to communicate with him.

19

The Pit Bull (American Staffordshire Terrier) has a vise-like grip. This dog—originally bred for fighting—often is poorly trained, inadequately controlled and has prompted legislation about protection dogs.

In reality, the owner was accomplishing exactly the opposite of what he was trying to do. Rather than calming and controlling the animal which should have viewed his owner as the "Pack Leader," this dog was encouraged by the shouts from a "Pack Member" who had never before demonstrated dominance over the dog. The dog perceived that the owner was taking part in the chase and adding fuel to the fire. Once the owner began to beat the dog another natural instinct was aroused in the dog—defense. While the child was under the dog something began to hurt the dog. Amidst the chaos of shouts, screams and violent physical contact the dog was now involved in a peer fight for the prey. Finally the dog was defeated by another pack member (his owner) for the prey. The defeated animal was forced from his territory, allowing the victor to claim the spoils.

It is clear that canine aggression in its natural form, guided only by the natural instincts of the dog is dangerous and undesirable. This quality of aggression imparts a great responsibility on the owner. It needs to be channeled and molded by the owner. For some people, this quality of natural aggression may need to be almost extinguished, and left only as a vocal remnant—the barking dog. For others willing to learn, train, and accept the responsibility, aggressive behavior can be an asset. Again we emphasize—CONTROL is the watchword. The dog's natural instincts that lead to aggression may be compared to fire, which uncontrolled will burn and destroy, yet when controlled provides the heat for our comfort. Very few of us require a dangerous inferno to heat our homes. Very few of us really need a biting dog.

We describe this biting dog as *"the real thing."* We do not encourage people to own dogs that will bite. To eliminate and avoid this behavior the dog must be trained. Biting is what dogs do naturally and control over this natural behavior is what we must obtain by training.

Dogs that will act aggressively are not for everyone. The most extreme form of dog aggression is determined attack and biting. Very few individuals actually require this type of dog for protection. It is absolutely imperative that those who do must accept the fact that the more aggression an individual dog will demonstrate the more responsibility his owner must assume. We cannot depend upon the dog's natural instincts to fluctuate in a manner to coincide with what we as *"rational"* beings need. The dog is not a *"moral"* animal.

In order to best promote a positive interaction, we must learn about the drives, motivations, and biologic reasons for canine protective

21

behavior. We need also examine our own motives for purchasing a dog for protection and understand what we really expect of him. What we expect of him will direct us to the degree of protection that we actually desire.

What is a protective dog? The definitions of a protective dog vary with the needs of the owner. Protection for some owners is a dog that alerts them when something unusual or threatening occurs. This is particularly important to the elderly or those with impaired hearing or sight. This protective dog is a sound alert dog. Truly important rescues have been made by the timely barking of this type of protection dog.

Sound alert dogs have been awarded commendations and newspaper acclaim. This is the dog that barks unceasingly at perceived danger. This dog may have been the one that, after training, was left with only the vocal remnant of aggression, or he may be a fearful dog, naturally inhibited to only sound an alert rather than confront a situation. Such dogs have warned their families or owners of such disparate threats as a Kodiak bear in Alaska trying to get into a fisherman's cabin or a fire breaking out in the sleeping family's apartment. The sound alert dog need not be of any specific breed. Small Terrier types are often ideal. Since the ability to protect is limited to the sound alert, the procedures required to enhance this quality of protective behavior are the least extensive.

As pleasing as it is for us humans to feel that our dog was trying to "protect" us from the bear or the fire, it probably isn't so! We cannot and should not ignore the fact that self protection and survival is always near the surface for the least confident dog. By his barking, howling, and whining this vocal dog is trying to protect himself. He seeks to enlist aid from the bigger, stronger, and more dominant members of his pack—his owners. Thus, if you are choosing a dog to serve as 'sound alert' protection, an aggressive, confident dog, may be the worst choice. Most of the time the strong, confident dog is often quieter and less quick to sound an alert. Fearful dogs are easily threatened, are often hyper-alert and quick to vocalize their concern. Common types of dogs that are recommended for sound alert duty are usually small, active, feisty, and as puppies are noticeably "yippy."

For some people protection means the dog's ability to deter by appearance. This category of protective dog requires that the dog "look vicious," whether he is or not. All that is required is form—not substance. The most extreme form of protection potential—the will-

CARE PACKAGE

ingness to bite—is often neither needed nor wanted. The "Gentle Giant" provides deterrence by his appearance. A biting dog, unfortunately, is often sought when protection obtained only by an intimidating appearance would suffice. Visual intimidation is best accomplished by what we will call the Gentle Giants.

The most extreme form of canine protection is afforded by "The Real Thing"—a biting, punishing, confident, pushing dog that requires tremendous input of training and commitment by his owner. True protection dogs have been grossly misunderstood by the public and are often wrongly characterized as vicious. We must not confuse a vicious dog with a trained attack dog.

Viciousness in a dog is uncontrolled behavior. It is what we, as movie-goers and television watchers, view as the canine actor—playing the villain—shows his teeth, growls gutturally, and with much fanfare attacks the hero without reason. A dog's growling, and showing of teeth, can be so fear-provoking that it blinds us to the motivation of his aggression. However, when Lassie behaves aggressively it isn't described as vicious because Lassie always has her reasons and is an excellent judge of human character. Moral judgments by dogs only happen in the movies, with a trainer's guidance.

This complicated behavior of aggressive display such as growling, is a result of an interplay of factors of temperament and environment. We have categorized reasons for aggression into the following: A. Territoriality, B. Suspicion, C. Play Drive, D. Courage, E. Hardness-Softness, and F. Sharpness.

Vicious behavior is always unwanted, uncontrolled, and often dangerously unexpected. Aggression that comes from the dog choosing to assert himself (and not in our behalf), is what we mean when we categorize a dog as 'vicious.' A vicious dog is one that bites your child, your neighbors child, or your friend. However, this same biting behavior, if directed at a mugger, midnight intruder, or threatening stranger, is identified as protectiveness or courage. Clearly then, one man's canine terrorist is another man's canine freedom fighter. Our task is to try to learn how these types of menacing displays originate and how they can be controlled and made to suit our purposes. As homeowners, apartment dwellers, and family members, training the right dog will provide a protector yet NOT involve us in litigation, sorrow, and guilt for what our dogs might do.

In order to elevate and develop protective behavior, it is necessary to understand what is the genetic and what is the learned basis of the protective dog's behavior so that the word vicious will be seen for what it is—a description of uncontrolled behavior. Juvenile delinquency is a description of uncontrolled behavior in youths. Vicious behavior in our dogs is the canine equivalent. Exaggeration of juvenile "hi-jinks" to the point where it causes injury or breaks the law finds its canine parallel in the extreme behavior of a dog out of control, the vicious dog. The juvenile delinquent might have become a productive member of society with a different environment and proper early training. The very qualities we look for in a puppy as a future protector can, with a different environment, produce the vicious dog.

Canine territoriality, suspicion, hardness and sharpness are the raw material which can be shaped by correct training into a thing of beauty and utility. However, this same dog will become vicious rather than protective if he is not trained or if his training is lax, indifferent, or even misdirected to encourage extreme aggressive behavior.

An example of lax canine supervision which leads to vicious behavior is the once inoffensive dog which seemingly "got mean" and began attacking children. Upon examination of these instances we find they are frequently present in a dog that has been tied or restrained, teased by children, and ignored by his owners. A dangerous pattern is set when the teasing terminates when the dog barks or acts aggressively. After the children have provoked, annoyed, and sprinted away from the barking dog for several days, the dog learns that his frustration can only be stopped by aggressive behavior which succeeds in chasing off his tormentors. This is an unfortunate duplication by the children of similar agitation methods used by professional protection dog trainers to encourage aggressive behavior. The courts are not expected to concern themselves with how a dog developed into this dangerous creature but are entrusted to protect the public from the 'vicious' dog. The reason for this aggressive behavior is irrelevant to the judge who orders the dog destroyed. And the surprised owners, who had purchased a 'nice' dog, can't understand why he got 'mean.'

A successful merging of characteristics of temperament is what we seek in a protective companion. If neglected, or misdirected, these same characteristics will produce a destructive, dangerous, and uncontrollable animal. This final product is made not born. What is so difficult to understand, and what some dog owners refuse to understand, is that lack of training can result in a vicious dog. Neglected and ignored dogs, just as children, do not suddenly turn bad!

There are many myths of how to "create" a vicious dog. Feeding them gunpowder, or repeated bouts of isolation will not create a vicious dog, only a sick and frightened one. Yet, the lack of correction/control of a dog's undesirable aggressive behavior such as growling or lunging will make the animal become what the courts describe as a vicious dog. Failure by the owner to control an assertive and aggressive canine personality will inevitably lead to an 'accident.' For a dog, as for a child, indifference to his activity is acceptance and reinforcement. Thus, confidence and aggression, if properly channeled, can produce the loving canine protector we want. However, when ignored, this same puppy can grow to become an unfortunate and dangerous canine liability. For anyone who is considering becoming a dog owner and yet is unwilling to accept the extensive training responsibilities of that ownership, an electronic burglar alarm would be a far better choice.

"Magic," the author's Giant Schnauzer, a good protection dog, is intimidating both in appearance and action.

Canine Motivation for Protection —
A Study of Temperament

Territoriality and The Fear Biter

Territoriality is the innate desire of a dog to defend the area in which he lives.. For his human companions, this is the most desirable motivation for defense. A dog with strong territorial instincts will bark, growl and place himself bodily in front of the entrance to his territory. The same dog, away from home, is often friendly and tolerant of strangers. He is confident about himself yet wary about those who enter his home. It is important that his behavior be distinguished from the "fear biter."

The "fear biter" is a dog of weak character who will also appear protectively aggressive in his home. When away from his home, such as in a park, the fear biter barks, growls and is aggressive at the approach of a stranger. The fear biter, is not confident and makes defensive displays no matter where he is because he is always protecting HIMSELF. The territorial dog in contrast to this frightened neurotic flasher of teeth does not threaten when away from his home. It is the unstable and fearful dog who, when he is away from his territory, threatens a child or passerby who walks near him. The dog, displaying pure territorial aggression, knows the difference between being protective at home and being taken for a walk on neutral ground. The territorial dog IS the sensible protector—stable, confident and alert.

A simple test for territoriality is having a stranger approach the dog on his home ground. The family car, yard, or in the home would be excellent examples of his territory. The ideal response should be barking and aggressive behavior which increases as the stranger approaches and decreases if they withdraw. In contrast this same dog if taken for a walk should appear indifferent, aloof or disinterested to the same stranger. Spontaneous aggressive behavior is extremely undesirable if it occurs away from the dog's home. Uncontrolled, and often unexpected aggression usually identifies a fear biter.

The fear biter's behavior in a household will show constant alertness to anyone who has entered the home, aggressive growling at movement of any guest, flashing of teeth at sudden movement by unfamiliar adults or children, and attempted or actual nips and bites as people walk away from the dog. This dog is commonly mistaken for the "perfect" home protector. Untrained, the fear biter will not stand his ground when threatened. Vigorous stamping of the feet or shouting can transform this growling menace into a fleeing coward.

Alfi, a German Shepherd bitch, was a classic fear biter. If a guest would come to our home she would throw herself against the door growling and barking. She had to be restrained in order for guests to enter our house. Once inside guests were constantly under her strict surveillance—one quick move and she sprang at them growling and biting. Within about thirty minutes she would quiet down, but continue to be observant and wary. If a child or adult stood up she would begin to growl again. On numerous occasions, when unrestrained, she would nip as they turned away from her. This dog was fearful to the extreme and displayed aggressive behavior in an effort to threaten all that she feared. Her behavior did not change whether she was traveling in a car, being walked, shown at a dog show, or at the veterinarian. She would not tolerate being touched or approached. Her behavior was thus stereotyped and she gave the same threatening response no matter what the stimulus. A child's outstretched palm or an adult overtly threatening her with a baseball bat caused the same growl and showing of teeth.

Because of Alfi's tremendous aggressive displays we sought to test her intensity to protect. We left the house and arranged for one of our friends dressed in full protective gear to break into our home. As he turned the knob of the unlocked door Alfi exploded into a barking rage. As the door was opened Alfi stood ten feet from the door continuing her aggression. Before the intruder could make a threatening gesture to test Alfi, she began to back up at his approach. He continued to walk confidently toward her and spoke quietly. As he approached, Alfi broke and ran, breaking through the rear door of the house and escaping into the outdoors in a panic. She continued to run and it took our best efforts for the next half hour to coax her back into our home.

Magic is a Giant Schnauzer who has spent his life being a children's toy. He serves as a pony, pillow, and the subject of all sorts of children's games played by three rambunctious boys, aged five, eight, and eleven. Magic is a good friend of the children's playmates, and when walked, will offer a friendly lick to anyone interested in making friends. Magic, however, does not permit unfamiliar adults to enter his home. When a stranger arrives at the door, Magic appears much the same as Alfi. However, because of training, if commanded to stop Magic will permit the stranger to enter and will then lie down obediently. If a sudden move or loud noise is made by the stranger, it will draw his attention but will not result in an aggressive outburst.

Magic has been tested as was Alfi. He could not be made to retreat. When attempts were made to frighten him off he became more aggressive. Finally when the stranger refused to leave and became more aggressive by waving a plastic ball bat, Magic attacked with ferocity. Thirty minutes later, the intruder and Magic's owner together re-entered the home. Magic lay quietly next to his owner as if the preceding scenario had never occurred.

As these examples indicate, aggressive behavior can be shown by either a stable confident animal or a fearful and unsteady animal. The display will look the same, but the motivation is quite different.

Territoriality in a dog that is confident is the MOST EFFECTIVE and safest choice for home protection. The fear biter will warn you, then run if his warning isn't effective. The fear biter will often bite a stranger who runs away, even if he is an invited guest. The trained territorial protector will protect his home, yet remain manageable and safe when strangers are invited in. A dog which is neither a fear biter nor a territorial protector will be blissfully uncaring about whoever comes in late at night and seeks to part your hair with an ax.

Territoriality is a fundamental aspect of the competent protection dog's temperament. Your home, yard, automobile is your dog's territory. It contains the people, things, scents, sights, and sounds which are familiar and comfortable. It is a place of security and comfort for the dog.

Most dogs possess some degree of territoriality but the drive must be strong to be of use and the dog confident enough to express it. Frequently a territorial dog is so submissive to humans that he will not protect his property against them, but he will protect against intruding dogs. Obviously, we are not concerned about being burglarized by a gang of criminal dogs! Only dogs who feel comfortable showing aggression against human intruders make suitable protectors. Some breeds of dogs are significantly less apt to challenge an invading human. Typically these are dogs specially bred for non-protective activities. For example, those breeds which were genetically bred to chase prey by sight (Greyhound, Saluki, Whippet) are not typically thought of as being territorial. Neither are many sporting dogs bred for retrieving or flushing game.

This characteristic of territoriality is independent of the dog's size. The breeds of dog that are usually strongly territorial are often the same dogs which one would consider working dogs and herding dogs. These breeds were genetically produced to look after herds, flocks, people, and geographic areas. Characteristics that were specifically emphasized by early breeders were the ability and desire to drive out marauding animals, other dogs, or anyone that might endanger the property of the owner which the dog considered to be within his territory. Thus was developed the modern guard dog and police types such as the German Shepherd, Doberman, Rottweiler, Bouvier de Flandres, and the Giant Schnauzer.

One dog's territory may be as small as his sleeping space and area around his food bowl. Yet the other extreme can include a dog who views all he surveys as his territory. It is not uncommon for a farm dog to view all six hundred forty acres of his owner's farm as his own yard, and he will never recognize the transfer or change of ownership of that property regardless of new fence boundaries.

Similarly, a territorial dog that is the canine pioneer in the first house of a subdivision, often will claim a very large area. Difficulties can arise when subsequent neighbors and their pets move into the area which the first dog had determined was his territory. No matter how long the later arrivals live in the subdivision, they will always be perceived as intruders by the first resident, resulting in barking, dog fights, and canine territorial marking contests.

The breeds that are inherently territorial are often easiest to develop from puppyhood into adult home protectors. This does not preclude other breeds of dogs from being territorial protectors—particularly the large Terriers, other working breeds, or even various mixed breeds. But just as one would have difficulty finding other breeds or mixed breeds that could outrun the Greyhound, so is it difficult to consistently find members of other breeds with more aptitude for territorial protection than these former herding dogs.

Suspicion

Suspicion is a characteristic in dogs which is often considered un-American. Everyone likes a dog in someone else's home to be "friendly." This friendliness is more accurately described as an exuberant welcome extended by the dog to any new person in the house. It would be a disaster if a family's protector responded with instant acceptance of a new person entering his home at night by breaking through a glass door.

Certainly friendliness can range from charming to obnoxious depending upon whether the dog merely wags his tail or knocks you down as he refuses to take NO for an answer as he mops you with his drooling, loving muzzle. For obvious reasons, this friendliness is not what is wanted in a protective dog. We are looking for a dog that demonstrates alertness but discretion when meeting strangers. Those who are unfamiliar to the dog are not to be immediately trusted. Be prepared, suspicion by the canine member of your home will not be looked upon by your friends in a positive manner. Several breed standards describe the dogs personality as "aloof." The dictionary defines aloof as being withdrawn, disinterested, unsympathetic, reserved. Visiting strangers to your home will wonder why their kissing sounds, clucking and attempts at petting are received with a baleful glance. The aloof and suspicious animal does not lavish his affection on just anyone.

Suspicion, typically, is not demonstrated by the puppy. When seen at a very young age, timidity is often mistakenly confused with suspicion. Thus, a fishy glance or attempts to avoid human contact by a young puppy should be considered undesirable reactions. A young puppy should be confident and playfully aggressive toward strangers.

Characteristics such as suspicion require potential protection dog owners to examine their own lifestyle. For some people a protection dog is not a realistic consideration if their home life requires their dog to be friendly with all visitors. Contrary to Hollywood logic, it is extremely unusual for a dog to selectively demonstrate aggressive behavior toward the "bad guys" and be friendly with all others. In reality the family dog will greet both friends and strangers with equal acceptance and affection. This obviously precludes protectiveness in the home.

This tied out Doberman is a fear biter.

As the photographer approached, the Doberman panicked and attacked.

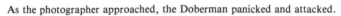

Suspicion is fundamental for the home protector. This suspicion may be displayed by the frantic barking of the SOUND ALERT dog, the baritone baying of the GENTLE GIANT or the cobra-like stare of the REAL THING. A potential protection dog owner, regardless of the degree of protection required, cannot expect that the dog can somehow judge the difference between the good guy and the bad guy. Dogs do not have a sixth sense to detect evil in the heart of the nocturnal visitor. Frequently we are disillusioned by the realization that a protective dog will distrust EVERY stranger who enters his territory. This protector inherently must have a sense of uneasiness about people in his territory and should not show instant acceptance of your new boyfriend, girlfriend, babysitter, boss' wife, or your Aunt Tilly—who raises miniature Poodles and knows all about dogs. The home protector is not there to win friends—he is there to influence people!

This quality of suspicion, distrust, or fear is one of the most difficult to deal with when choosing a 'working' protector. In its extreme, this characteristic is not a virtue, and can cause untold misery for the person who obtains a dog whose suspicious character disrupts normal household routine. The intensely suspicious dog threatens attacks on all newcomers, be they small children, grown men, or your neighbor whom he has seen for the thirtieth time this month. He does not like or trust anyone except those in his household.

Often individuals, particularly after being victims of a crime or in the immediate vicinity of a violent criminal act, say they want the REAL THING, a biting dog that is intensely suspicious, ferocious as well as savage. In many states a three day waiting period (cooling off time) is mandatory for taking possession of a firearm. Similar caution should be exercised when seeking a dog for security reasons. Don't buy on emotion! We have delayed delivery of this type animal and found that, when sweet reason returned, a SOUND ALERT dog that barked as an expression of his suspicion to strangers was all that was required.

A man called and explained that he and his wife had suffered two "break and enter" attempts at their home within the past two days. His wife had been at home each time—she was terrified. The robbers consisted of two different groups of four individuals. It was never determined if the motive was to assault her or to burglarize the home. The couple had resided at this location for the past ten years without incident. His wife was petrified at the thought of staying at home

33

alone. The police suggested that they get a nasty guard dog. They came to look at dogs, declaring that their situation was authentic and that only a truly effective dog would do—they wanted the REAL THING. This would be their first dog, and they wanted the best. They demanded a dog that would "do the job." We attempted to explain the impossibility of bringing a grown, trained protective dog into their home as their first dog. The tenacity of a protective male would be beyond their control. I selected a female who was skillfully obedience trained and had previously lived in a home with small children—the perfect dog for them! They didn't think she sounded like enough dog for the job, but condescended to look at her. In the process of getting acquainted the dog playfully nipped the woman's trouser knee when she petted her. The woman became hysterical and was terrified of the dog which had to be removed from her presence. Any intentions of purchasing a grown dog were quickly forgotten.

This situation was unfortunate, yet typical of the wide spread misunderstanding of protective dog behavior. If this couple could have purchased the REAL THING their worries about intruders would have been replaced by the fear of domination and even an attack upon them by their 'protector.'

A word of caution—the poorly informed, impulsive buyer may be sold an unsocialized "kennelized dog" represented as a protection animal. Too often this behavior has been induced in the animal by neglect. He has been raised without adequate human contact during the early formative months of development. He acts much as a wild animal fearing all that he sees and expressing this fear either by withdrawal or, if his exit is blocked, by the frantic aggression of a trapped animal—a fear biter. Certainly this form of suspicion, displayed to the extreme by the dog, is valueless for someone wishing anything other than a dog to be kept as a wild animal confined on the property. Therefore, we seek modification in the development of suspicion and by socialization and training which builds confidence in the animal. The young pup must be exposed to many situations including automobiles, people, and other animals to allow him a normal psychic development. We cannot emphasize too strongly that total isolation of the young pup, in order to make the good watch dog, will usually result in a potentially dangerous psychologically crippled canine.

Socialization

Socialization is the modification of inherent characteristics of the dog by exposure to our human world. Simply stated we want the dog to think he is a person! It is a form of training. It can be informal by simply permitting the dog to observe and interact with his owners—growing up in the home. The owner may emphasize what is cause for suspicion and what is not. He can accomplish this by reward and correction. For example when the dog identifies a stranger approaching the house and gives a barking alert he should be praised and reassured. This praise and reassurance can help him develop confidence in determining what should be barked at. Similarly, barking directed at small children should be stopped. This may require the withdrawal of praise as well as formal correction such as a determined collar jerk. Socialization will direct the development of the dogs personality to produce the correct protective dog for a specific family.

Play Drive

A lethargic animal that would rather not lift more than an eyelid as someone comes to the door, could hardly be expected to serve as a front line of defense. A normal to high energy level is easily evaluated by observing the puppy's desire for play. It is the frisky puppy or energetic adult dog that wants to chase a ball, nip at your heels and jump a fence, who will also have the energy and interest to protect both himself and you. By the same token we can see certain types of dogs eliminated as potential protective dogs regardless of their size or ominous appearance when they act lazy, or are just not interested. Without being overly negative, certain ponderous breeds will provide an element of protection simply by the physical intimidation of their size. However, one must realize they usually are all show and no go. Of course there are always exceptions, but for the first-time dog owner the likelihood of success in obtaining a protective companion within the generally ponderous and lethargic breeds is not high. Correspondingly, those dogs that appear feisty, are live wires, and are active with high play drive, will be at the door at three a.m. when someone attempts to break in.

An important concept of play drive relates to the mechanism of prey-chasing in dogs. The play (prey) drive can often be evaluated in young dogs by their desire to chase a ball, nip at your heels, run after a

The body posture of this dog is a giveaway. The tucked tail shows it is "fear" that motivated this animal.

butterfly, or in the beginning form of protection training, trying to grasp and hold on to an object they are teased with such as a burlap sack or towel. This play (prey) drive has been used effectively to develop real protection dogs when modified by combining it with the dog's desire to catch his prey and to protect himself. Prey training will be expanded upon during discussion of methods of training a protection dog.

Fear biter. This face shows both fear and aggression. The dog is on the panic, ready to bite or run.

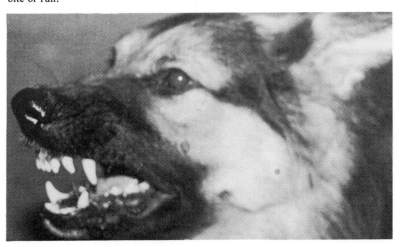

Courage

We all tend to wrap our dog friends with cloaks of human emotion. It is for this reason that we often describe characteristics of dogs in terms of emotions or feelings that we understand. Courage is just such an emotion, and it is one the public identifies with security or police dogs.

To the best of our knowledge, dogs, unlike people, cannot imagine their own death. There is significant controversy among experts as to whether a dog will enter a situation willingly in which he has previously experienced as having been injurious, painful or merely disagreeable. Why then, you may ask, will a police dog attack an oncoming armed or threatening felon? Fundamental to understanding seemingly courageous behavior of a police dog bearing down on an assailant firing a gun at him, is an understanding of the difference between canine and human behavior. Unlike a man, the dog is unaware that the noise can do him harm. The threat of a firearm would immobilize most people yet this threat is not perceived by the dog. To compare a man's decision to face gunfire with a dog's decision to charge forward regardless of the noise, is the worst sort of anthropomorphism. In order to utilize a protection or working dog we must understand his very different origin. The fundamental aspect of all serious protection dog training (biting dogs) is the building of the dog's confidence. Dogs being trained for physical confrontation with men NEVER lose in practice situations. Very carefully and in graduated series of encounters the dog is shown that his behavior by barking, lunging, and even biting always results in victory. To accomplish this the human being participating in these examples of man-dog confrontation will always assume the role of the loser. The dog always wins!

Hardness and Softness

In conversations between dog trainers, one hears discussion of the hardness of their dogs and how sympathetic they are about the softness of their colleague's dog. The macho position is that their dog is very hard and tough as nails. What does "hard" really mean? It corresponds to a stubbornness, determination, a tenacity of the dog to do what he wishes, when he wishes, sometimes despite painful correction. Conversely, the soft dog is easily dissuaded from doing what he wishes, often by only the spoken word. You may surmise anyone seeking a protective dog would initially think 'the harder the better.'

The difficulty arises when hardness becomes a problem in training. An example of a hard dog would be a dog that chases cars, gets hit, is hospitalized, recovers and returns home to continue to chase cars as if nothing had happened. The hard security dog can be useful whenever a situation arises that requires that the dog work alone and be subject to abuse from an aggressor. In a household situation, the advantages of hardness are lost when attempts to train fail or when training requires corrections that the owner is unwilling to make. It is then a desirable compromise to obtain a dog whose confidence can be developed and whose determination is such that he can carry out the tasks asked of him despite distraction or even resistance.

Trainability must be a part of the hard dog. His hardness cannot be so extreme that he is insensitive to all correction. Hardness to the extreme has been genetically produced in some breeds of dog. This hardness or ability to withstand pain and continue to fight or dominate is characteristic of the "pit" or "fighting" dogs.

Sharpness

Sharpness is a characteristic of dog behavior usually spoken of in the context of shy-sharpness. The sharp disposition is thought to be the mature product of the fear biter puppy. The mature shy-sharp dog may become so aggressive that he can be mistaken for a strong confident animal which is exhibiting dominance or territorial behavior. His fear is camouflaged by aggressive display. However by testing this dog, as was mentioned in the section on "territoriality," his true motivation becomes obvious when confronted in his territory by a confident intruder. The sharp dog will not bite when his bark doesn't stop the invader. He retreats growling. In this context, sharpness means the likelihood of biting when cornered or confronted. Do not confuse a sharp animal with a confident one. Sharpness in human beings would be deemed irritability. When an insecure dog is confronted with the unknown or what he perceives as potentially hostile, he will seek to withdraw. As the dog matures he will find, as do men, many fear-producing situations from which he cannot withdraw. He can then learn to deal with insecurity through another mechanism— aggressive posturing and behavior—rather than withdrawal. The degree to which this adaptation is successful is quite naturally dependent upon the dog's size and his appearance. A large dog or one recognized by the public as a police-type animal, will quickly find that his aggressive displays are met with withdrawal and fearful stance by strangers. He is encouraged to "put on" his aggressive display more frequently and with increasing vigor. The threshold for these displays is inversely proportional to the sharpness of the animal. Professional trainers have long realized that when a sharp dog is corrected from acting aggressively with training, the dog reverts to his fearful basic personality. A sharp animal when his bluff is called may slink, tuck tail and suddenly appear quite submissive.

Sharpness is the irritability threshold at which point a dog will "annoyance bite." We must not confuse an annoyance bite with an attack on a burglar, head on. The "annoyance bite" is a bite in the seat of the pants as the person walks or runs away, or a bite on the hand as an individual reaches out to pet the dog. Irritability is a reaction by the dog to a perceived threat. Thus a very sharp dog may strike out to bite a child running close to him in the periphery of his vision, while the less sharp dog may simply rotate his head to determine what this blur of motion is.

Sharpness is frequently associated with the fear biter. We have found that there is an almost constant relationship between the least confident, most fearful dogs and the likelihood that they will surprise the mailman or guest in your home with a sneak bite. Even the owner of an extremely sharp dog can be bitten by his dog if the dog is accidentally startled.

There is a value to sharp dogs. Despite their liabilities they are certainly great 'showmen' and serve to intimidate would-be foes. Unfortunately, these same dogs are the ones most likely to bite anyone. It is the shy-sharp dog that, because of his insecurity, snaps at a child raising a stick, becomes aggressive with a fearful visitor to the house, and usually cannot be safely left unattended even for a moment at a public place. Unless one is comfortable with his hyper-alert, paranoid antics, the extremely sharp dog is not for most homes. Occasionally he can be integrated into the lifestyle of the single adult. This dog is most happy living as a recluse. The very sharp and fearful dog can be truly dangerous to anyone. Unfortunately, they are often sold as "attack" trained. In these instances great danger stalks the unwary purchaser.

ONE MAN DOG

Ripoffs, Myths, and Tall Tales

The study and training of dogs is a field which would seem to encourage the establishment of instant experts. These instant authorities frequently make up exciting lies, stories, myths and fairy tales of canine lore. These myths are often entertaining but provide little substance for the selection, training, and understanding of our dogs. We would like to review some of the most common statements that "everybody knows."

One Man Dog

One of the most appealing myths for stroking our human ego, is that a dog will be loyal only to us and to no one else—FOREVER. In reality, this canine fidelity is something that can only happen under the most extreme and unusual circumstances. Its rarity is such that when it does truly occur and is documented it can warrant a monument, as has happened in Japan. In that instance, a dog would not leave the train station where he waited for a master who never returned. This dog had for many years waited daily at the station for his master to return from work. This routine was interrupted by his master's untimely death, yet the dog continued to wait. His vigil could not be interrupted by luring the dog with food or kind words—he died waiting. Even this honored observation of a dog's devotion has been challenged as anthropomorphism. A stereotyped or ritualistic canine behavior may be a mistaken concept.

The realistic understanding that one must have, no matter how deflating it is to our pride, is that our house pet or family protector will, within a few weeks, if treated kindly, accommodate to another home. He will become that family's protector and companion. He is not fickle, he is a dog!

We have taken delivery of dogs from Europe who have had years of close relationship with a single trainer and were under his training for serious police work. These strong, trained animals readily adapted to their new home and when given orders in German from a new master, responded crisply and with a desire to please. The one-man dog, if such truly exists, is extremely rare and one must wonder what benefits this quality would provide. It is a guarantee for disappointment to have false expectations with regard to our canine companions eternal fidelity. No, they will not wither and die if removed from the warm light of our companionship, but will readily adjust to a new pack leader provided the circumstances of their new home are favorable and realistic.

In general, dogs are very adaptable to accepting a change of owners. When they do not accept a change of ownership it may be due to a problem in the dog's temperament. We recall one dog, "Prince," who was boarded at our kennel and despite every attempt we made to feed him, spent a full week without eating. Prince rarely slept, never moved to potty, and was never seen standing. It certainly seemed that this dog was pining away for his owner. Everyone at the kennel tried again and again to comfort him. When kennel personnel tried to pet or comfort Prince he growled and snapped his warning to "stay away." When Prince was delivered home after his stay we expected him to give his owner an exuberant greeting. Instead Prince bit her! Prince's owner asked that we carry Prince, still in his crate, into the house because he was not leash broken. Inside the house, she tried again to remove Prince from the crate. Again he growled and didn't budge. Finally we disassembled the crate and "dumped" Prince from it. His owner then explained that Prince would retreat to the basement as soon as possible. When we told her of Prince's disturbing behavior at the kennel she said she wasn't surprised. The dog rarely associated with anyone, and spent most of his life in isolation in her basement. When Prince was at the kennel he missed the security of his basement "den."

Prince was the product of lack of socialization. His owner said that she purchased him in order to have a guard dog. She raised him exactly as suggested by the seller. Prince was never allowed to visit with strangers, rarely removed from the home and discouraged from dog/human games such as ball retrieval. Prince was routinely kept in the basement when strangers were in the house and placed in the basement when the owner was away. We had boarded Prince for the first time in his life when he was three years old. Needless to say Prince was NOT and would never become a guard dog. For that matter, Prince was of less value than a house plant, as he required more attention and provided even less companionship.

We have not been exempt from thinking that our dogs would maintain their undying loyalty to us—worrying that they could not tolerate our absence. One of our dogs, "Nick," was inseparable from me, his master. This German Shepherd was in every sense a "one-man dog." Nick's bond with me was so strong that whenever possible he was at my side. He would climb stairs, enter a vehicle, go up on a roof or climb a ladder in order to be with me. He loved me and WOULD NOT accept a correction or command given him by anyone else. When Nick's training was complete he was sold to a police officer as a working police dog. It was with great astonishment that I learned from Nick's new owner how quickly the dog had bonded to him, and how enthusiastically Nick obeyed only his commands. Nick had found a new pack leader in twenty-four hours.

Movie dogs

All of us have our own idea what constitutes the perfect dog. For the novice owner this impression is always to some degree molded by childhood memories of the celluloid heroes of the screen. Whether it was a German Shepherd, a Collie, or a Mutt, this movie dog, so well-remembered, could understand English, could reason, and compete successfully with human beings. The dog often seemed stronger, smarter (alerting the family to a danger they did not see), or purer of heart than the shallow human beings around him. In these dramas, human beings served as the supporting cast.

Examination of this cinematic fantasy from a dog trainer's point of view makes certain things obvious. Each of the scenes showing the dog doing something wonderful, such as jumping through flames, swimming a raging river, riding a horse, counting, were simply obedience routines taught to one of a number of dogs that were taking their turn portraying the canine star. Tricks of movie angles, film splicing, and cooperative stunt men lent further drama to our canine actor's scenes. Dogs as portrayed in movies of this type do not exist and never did. We should not realistically expect to find a dog which can out-reason us, do an instant character evaluation to identify the bad guy, or act as a ferocious guardian and fifteen minutes later have strangers petting, embracing and congratulating him for his most recent act of heroism.

In these romanticized canine, fantasy movies, no one has to scold the dog for pooping in the house, chewing on the furniture, or barking incessantly. On-screen television and movie dogs are not photographed while experiencing these rather common real life canine problems. Errors of behavior, accidentally caught by the camera, are edited out and left on the cutting room floor.

MOVIE DOG

Imported Dogs

In the last ten years we have witnessed in the United States the phenomenon that, "If it's from over there (Germany for example), it has got to be good." This belief has included automobiles, cameras, watches, and dogs. The dogs in question are usually from 'Herr So and So,' who has trained, bred, and shown Europe's most wonderful German Shepherds, or Rottweilers. A cousin, drinking buddy, or son who now lives in the United States will, for a small fee, import one of these "super dogs" for you. Will you get a canine Mercedes? Of course, the answer will be, "Yes," and you will be able to walk "super dog" across the Brooklyn bridge which someone also will be happy to sell you—on approval—for a nominal fee.

What can we really learn from the mystique of the imported protective dog? We should realize that for the last century in Europe there have been, in some cases, sincere attempts to improve the working ability, i.e. trainability and protective value of their stock. They have certainly been more successful in this regard than our native breeders who, for the most part, have different goals. In this country there is little in the way of organizational support for the working breeder which is available to the European breeder. Dog sport trials are so common in Germany as to make competitions a weekly event. Similar trials held in the United States occur with less than one tenth the frequency. The success of the German breeding program, however, has a nationalistic flavor. Fully trained animals of true merit, both in appearance and in character will cost many thousands of dollars. German breeders do not give their dogs away nor do they sell at bargain prices. Once the dog is shipped out of Germany, whether as a puppy or adult, there is no guarantee. Caveat Emptor (Buyer Beware) is the implicit assumption. The average person would do well to investigate locally, and certainly domestically, unless the importer is his drinking buddy or close relative. This somewhat cynical attitude is founded in our experience of having encountered many bilked, disappointed, and unhappy customers who bought a "pig in a poke."

Truly high-quality European animals are available but, to avoid making a costly—sometimes tragic—mistake you need someone you trust to select them, guarantee them, and show you how to train them. Dogs do not get trained and stay that way. Training is a continuing process that becomes part of the dog's relationship with his new owner.

If you attempt to purchase a "super dog" when you just happen to be in Europe you will find that language, custom, and limitations of time make an intelligent selection extremely difficult. We once spent several weeks in Europe entirely devoted to looking for excellent working animals. We looked at well over fifty dogs and returned with two grown dogs and one puppy!

Deadly Breeds—Devil Dog

Some of the greatest "bunk" occurs when people try to buy that special breed, "the devil dog." A dog promoted in this vein as a type of "devil dog" is guaranteed to be THE REAL THING. Sometimes the dog will be a specially crossed animal such as a Wolf/German Shepherd or a Doberman/German Shepherd. It even may be designated with a contrived name such as an "Alaskan Alsatian," or a "Dober-Shepherd."

Purchasers looking for such a dog vary from the movie-goer who has seen "that movie," to the consumer advocate who has studied breed descriptions of each dog, and come to the conclusion that the "Russian Tundra Wolfhound" is the ONLY animal that will suit his purposes. Sometimes a dog may become a "devil dog" simply by changing his name. One friendly protection dog dealer told us of an incredible 'lemon' that he owned which he could not sell under the name of "Blackie." He changed the dog's name to "Bad Finger," added a good story to go with him and had people lined up to buy him. He was promptly sold to the highest bidder.

Black dogs, big dogs, dogs named "Killer," "Assassin," "Man Hunter," "Devil," and "Damian," are usually presented as something special. A dog salesman once told me that German Shepherds with black faces are more "deadly" watch dogs as compared to those with light faces!

More often than not the "devil dog" will be a deranged, irrational lunatic who has a tendency to bite anyone and everyone including his owner—an uncontrollable FEAR BITER or an extremely dominant dog that was never trained to respect his owner.

Reports of the existence of such a breed are pure hype—there are no "devil dogs."

Going for the Throat

In many dog stories the vicious dog is depicted as "going for the throat" when attacking. This widespread myth is reinforced in movies and on television. During a dog attack, a person is knocked to the ground, and the dog is seen straddling the stunt man's chest with his head buried somewhere between the man's upper torso and face. Depending on the script, after ten seconds of this rather violent activity, punctuated by blood-thirsty growls, the man either lies limp or the dog has been shot. This doesn't happen in real life. In reviewing multiple dog bites inflicted during police work it has been demonstrated that, even in a street situation, the dog will bite anything he can reach—including such theatrically unappealing areas as buttocks, groin, foot, hand or arm.

The wolf, our dog's wild cousin, brings down game by biting at legs, underbelly, and eventually immobilizing his prey by causing the animal to collapse from exhaustion from multiple bites. Dogs are similar, they bite anywhere they can reach, and usually do not spring for the head or neck but rather bite at their own standing level. This behavior can be modified as seen in some of the illustrations showing dogs attacking a sleeve. In training situations the sleeve is brought higher and higher and the dog learns to reach up and bite at a higher level. The unhappy frequency of facial bites suffered by children result from their small stature and not the dog's malicious intent.

Champions

Everyone wants a breed champion—a "show dog." When purchasing a puppy you may encounter a seller who boasts that there are twenty-seven champions in the pup's pedigree. Terrific! So what, exactly, is a champion? What does it mean to have a pup with twenty-seven champions in his pedigree? In the United States, 'Champion' (Ch.) usually refers to a dog's accomplishments in the "show" ring at American Kennel Club or United Kennel Club dog shows. These competitions are designed to have a dog judge, one whom the AKC or UKC has officially declared to be familiar with that particular breed, decide which of the dogs appearing before him in the ring that day most closely resembles the description of the breed—as stated in official breed Standards in reference to physical appearance. The evaluation of character and temperament in this competition is comparable to the evaluation of character obtained by the questions offered to the beauty contestants in our favorite national pageants. What does the title tell you about a dog? Very little. Are there champions who can be superb working, protective companions? Yes, and

47

everyone wants THAT dog. This is like requiring (as a prerequisite to being a champion) that a big league professional baseball player must also be handsome, photogenic and have a great body as well as a great mind. There is nothing wrong with beauty in our dogs and this is certainly what seeking a champion should encourage. But beauty is often subject to interpretation (''eye of the beholder'') while protective

IMPORTED DOG

character and trainability are not. A championship title awarded to a particular dog is not a certificate of temperamental merit or even a guarantee of average intelligence, but rather an acknowledgement of aesthetic appeal and general conformation to the Standard of the breed, e. g., long ears, dark eyes, big feet—whatever. It is nice to own a dog like this if you want to brag that your dog is a 'Champion' and also if you are seeking to breed dogs and establish a line which looks the same—so they too can become champions.

One of the best examples of beautiful conformation evolving from breeding for function is the Thoroughbred horse. This breed was originally developed from a combination of Arabian stallions and English mares. Over the years tremendous emphasis was placed on speed as the criteria for selective breeding. It would be difficult to argue this animal is not a prime example of pure equine beauty. Just imagine how difficult it would be to breed this same speed and appearance while also stipulating that each animal have four white stockings and a white blaze on his forehead. This problem is present in dog breeding when coat length, color, texture, eye color, ear set, dentition, and presence or absence of a curl in the tail must be met to meet a particular Standard. Other aspects of the Standard relating to the skeletal structure and movement of the dog impact directly on his function and working ability. Physical appearance is important when it relates to and is designed for accomplishment of the activity for which a dog was originally bred. However, fads and fancies as well as just old fashioned politics do influence which dog becomes a champion. Eventually, if a fad persists (as in Cocker Spaniels), many changes are made in the dog's appearance for the show ring. A Cocker Spaniel in 'show coat,' groomed for the show ring, is presented to the judge with the flowing locks of his coat almost dragging on the floor. It would be ridiculous indeed if such a specimen were plunked down in a field of grasses and briars with the expectation that he could maneuver for upland game.

The temperament of the dog is not measured in the show ring beyond a superficial evaluation. This evaluation comes when the judge approaches and examines the dog. During this time the dog is in close contact with his handler, receiving reassurance from this physical contact and, if need be, correction by the handler if the dog tends to act "shy." Should the dog threaten the judge his temperament will be considered faulty and he will be excused from the ring. If

49

THE REAL THING

the dog attempts to avoid the judge, this 'shyness' may or may not be overlooked. If the dog actually bites or attempts to bite the judge, he could be disqualified from further appearance in the show ring at that show or any other. Nonetheless, it is not possible for a judge to ascertain the dog's basic temperament to any appreciable degree during the brief time spent determining relative standings in the conformation ring. For the most part, the judge makes his evaluation only of the dog's gait, coat, and other visual criteria described in the Standard for that breed.

Male vs. Female

During these times of the feminist movement we are happy to proclaim an equal opportunity for the female protective dog. The female of the species in the canine world has many advantages. True, some females may leave home temporarily but this is usually a seasonal event, and one that usually will not happen with neutered animals. (If your dog—male or female—is not in a position to leave your property, as should be the case, this problem is moot.)

The spayed female can be alert, confident and highly territorial. Though she does not often manifest the all out, straining-at-the-lead type of aggression of some males, this characteristic is rarely needed in an animal whose purpose is to defend hearth and home.

There are two aspects of the female dog that often permit all family members, including the children of the house, to interact more comfortably with her. The female's relatively smaller size and her often less dominant character makes her "fit in better" to the smaller living spaces of apartments, condos, and small homes. And the female will respond more sensitively to the non-alpha members of the home (mom and the kids).

The male dog is usually what we think of when we describe the professional attack dog, or a police dog. Review of dogs used by police, security services, the military, and others who require the most extreme form of aggression and intensity, show that these dogs are usually males. There are exceptions, but in most breeds the search for the serious female attack dog can be an exhausting endeavor. An 'attack' level of aggression is not needed by the vast majority of people seeking protective animals and the 'sound alert dog' can easily be of either sex. The 'gentle giant' is often one hundred and fifty pounds in the female version and more in the male. But, not much is gained with an extra seventy-five pounds of overkill in your home. Thus, short of an actual need for the serious attack-trained animal, we tend to favor females for home protection. A male dog will frequently challenge his owner, and will make attempts to assert himself. The concept of a dog "turning on his master" is in many instances another way of describing the adolescent male dominance displays of an energetic pup. The first time an inexperienced owner encounters this he may worsen the situation by avoiding conflict with the dog. Often the owner will let the dog do what he likes until the situation becomes unmanageable. A young male that establishes his dominance over his owner usually becomes the dangerous adult that attacks his owner. Such problems are far less frequent with females.

After many years as professional dog trainers, we are acutely aware that **ALMOST ALL** of the family aggression problem dogs—those who bite family members—are male dogs. The dog has become dominant, the pack leader, and has subjugated by fear the rest of his human family. This is the major reason why we normally recommend a female dog for a family.

Males belonging to the protective breeds are not for the average dog/pet owner. A frequent complaint from an owner of a male protection dog is, "I wanted a canine family member that would be a loveable pet and protector, NOT the dog I got who requires constant supervision and serious correction."

Dog Aggression vs. People Aggression

At dog shows, in parks, or on your own block, we have all seen dogs displaying aggression to other dogs—dog fighters. Sometimes this is repetitive behavior and we know that a certain dog is a well-recognized bully. Is this 'dog-fighter' an optimal protection animal? NO. Absolutely not!

In Europe, protection dogs are often tested by being faced with a human aggressor while twenty yards in front of that aggressor lies a large dog. It is a disqualifying fault of the dog being tested should he run toward, sniff, or show any aggression or interest in this animal rather than attacking the human antagonist.

In similar fashion, we witnessed tests of the ATTS (American Temperament Testing Society) in which all types of dogs are presented with a standardized series of encounters including a friendly stranger, neutral stranger, and a frankly hostile stranger. There was no correlation between the behavior of the dog in these encounters and his level of aggression to other dogs who are waiting to be tested. Dogs that are described as dog-fighters—certain Terriers, and others which could be best described as "pit animals," are often indifferent to the human confronting them. This does not mean that such dogs could not be trained to be sensitive to human events around them, but it is a great mistake for us to believe that dog aggression is a positive indicator that they would be protective to our home and family.

We have had people bring dogs for protection training with exceedingly high expectations based on how ferocious the animal had been to their neighbor's dog. These expectations are almost always mercilessly shattered as the ferocious "dog bully" cowers behind his master when he is shouted at or threatened. These people, if they sincerely want to try to continue training with this animal, must be made to understand that their dog will have to be reprogrammed.

Junk Yard Dog

Many have had the experience of coming up to a commercial building, industrial park or warehouse area only to find a very angry-appearing dog, running a fence, warning them not to enter. This is a security or guard dog and he is an animal that usually has had the least training and probably is endowed with an unstable character. His actions can be thought of as "protecting himself in his own territory." He is the classic "junk yard dog." This dog is usually a fear biter encouraged to act aggressively. This is not to say that these animals would not attack anyone climbing the fence, but in other respects they are wholly unsuitable for human, personal protection. These dogs do not accept close proximity of people and act aggressively to force them away. Some unscrupulous dealers attempt to sell these as "home guards." They are rarely house broken. They show no discretion—it is equally likely that they will attack a two year old child or an adult — and they are usually the product of indiscriminate breeding and inadequate socialization. Rather than being aggressive and confident animals, they are fearful and have learned to show aggressive displays in order to frighten off that which alarms them. Paradoxically, as this dog's fear intensifies, he will bite and withdraw rather than press a serious attack. Typically, this dog delivers a bite to the retreating side of a person. The bite is in the buttocks, calf, or foot, and is delivered as long as the subject is escaping. Such a dog would be dropped from a good police dog training program and would not be able to handle the rigors of Schutzhund protection work.

The dog behind the fence is not likely to be a gem. Even if the price was cheap, you probably paid too much.

Where not to buy your dog.

Classifications of Dogs, and Where to Purchase

The Sound Alert Dog

To purchase a protective dog, you must first evaluate your personal requirements. The degree of protection that you will require and the commitment you are willing to make as a trainer, will dictate the breed, size, sex, and inherent temperament of the dog to be purchased.

Most people will, after careful consideration, realize that what they need is a canine companion who will protect them by alerting them to anything that is unusual or threatening. This animal will accomplish his purpose by barking. The dog which "alerts" by barking needs the least training and is the easiest to obtain. We call this a "sound alert" dog. The sound alert dog can be of any size, breed or color. We have found that small active breeds of dogs are of value, as they tend to be 'yippie.'

We owned a female Manchester Terrier named Trixi. The lady of the house was very comforted, as Trixi would bark at the approach of a strange car in the driveway, remain quiet unless someone entered the yard, and throughout her fourteen years of life was a reliable protector. Her bark became so familiar, that though she was lost for several days, she could be heard when we went to the dog pound and recognized her bark from the hundreds of other animals in the shelter. Trixi certainly was not an attack animal, but she was an important asset to our "big city" living. Her barking became a standard by which our family could tell if someone strange was approaching the house. The several days that she was gone seemed much longer, as we not only missed her companionship but felt insecure in the absence of our canine sentinel.

When choosing your sound alert puppy it is to your advantage to observe how the breeder's personal dogs behave when you approach his residence. If you are at the breeder's home and are able to enter the house without any of the animals barking an alert, you might as well bid a polite goodbye. You should expect to hear dog(s) barking at your approach and that these same animals can be quieted easily by their owner as you are invited into their home. If the dog(s) must be removed before you enter the home then something may be wrong. Shy-sharp dogs, ones that are likely to bite, are often removed as visitors approach. These dogs bark out of fear and their fear is not easily allayed. For that reason, they are taken from your view. Their puppies, like all puppies, are cute and adorable. When these puppies mature, their inherited temperament will require close supervision. Often they become a liability and therefore should not be considered as a suitable choice.

One exception to this rule of eliminating from consideration a dog which has been removed when you visit is a bitch nursing her litter. This mother is uneasy with strangers in the house, particularly if she is kept away from her litter. As the litter matures, the mother becomes less possessive and anxious about the puppies. By six weeks, she is no longer nursing and her behavior should be back to normal.

The distinction between a 'sound alert' dog and a potentially dangerous 'shy-sharp' animal was made painfully clear to us. We were invited to see an eight-week-old litter of puppies of which both parents were "Conformation Champions." As we approached, the bitch was held on a tight leash by her owner and continued to whine, bark, and growl while we were speaking. I asked that the dog be put away before our children visited the litter. I was assured that although the bitch was a "watch" dog she was very good around children. I insisted anyway and she was dragged, while barking and whining, to the basement. Later, after we had visited the puppies and were in another part of the house, a different member of the household returned home and let the bitch out of the basement. She ran up the stairs and bit the visiting seven year old in the face. This behavior was one which clearly demonstrated instability and obviously ruled out this litter. Although the maternal drive is strong, it was inappropriate in this circumstance. Unfortunately, what many people describe as a "watch dog" is a fearful animal that is unpredictable and often will bite a child and/or adult impulsively.

What are we really looking for in the parents of a 'sound alert' dog? Active vocal dogs who bark behind a door, fence, or window and do not retreat when you enter the home are desirable candidates. The parents should not attempt to attack once you are invited/accepted into the house. It should never be necessary to drag the dog away from a visitor, nor should they show an unmanageable snapping, snarling, or lunging display. A very positive sign would be that the owner can, with a command, quiet the dog. If you purchase a puppy from a pet shop or animal shelter, in all likelihood, it will not be possible for you to get a look at the behavior or appearance of the parents of the puppy. You will be making a random selection—picking a puppy out of a hat. If you consider that you are looking for a dog (not a permanent puppy) who will be around your home for a decade or more, you may not want to gamble unnecessarily.

The Gentle Giant

A variant of the sound alert dog is the dog that announces a stranger's presence in a basso profunda that shakes the rafters, vibrates glass panes, and informs your neighbors within a quarter mile that someone has come to your house. This animal by necessity must be large and he combines the ability to alert and vocally intimidate. These huge dogs are increasing in popularity as their lion-like appearance and their deep barking is usually all that is needed to discourage would-be bad guys. Even though the head and bark may remind one of the MGM lion, this dog can be a real Mr. Milquetoast—a pussycat in guard dog's clothing. There is much to be said for this animal. Because of his threatening appearance he, just as the heavily muscled, tattooed, shirt-sleeve-bulging, ex-marine, rarely needs to exhibit any real aggressive behavior to make his point. This type of dog is what we call the 'Gentle Giant.' Breed examples of Gentle Giants are Saint Bernard, Great Dane, Mastiff, Newfoundland, or any of their bear-like mixtures.

The large sound alert dog provides a wonderful security blanket for those of us too lazy, too inept, or just not inclined to own a biting dog. This is often a blessing because a biting dog can often be a real liability. The majority of large sound alert dogs can often be obtained inexpensively from show breeders specializing in the large breeds. They will sell you a dog that is not suitable for the show ring and is described as "pet quality." Pet quality dogs may be sold with a neutering contract which serves to prevent you from reproducing whatever physical flaw that eliminated the dog from the show ring. This flaw is usually something such as incorrect color, height, improper angulation, or cryptorchidism—flaws that would not interfere with his duties as a watch dog or family member.

Dog Shows are wonderful places to observe contrasting levels of activity, canine curiosity, tendency for barking, and response to strangers. A serious error can be made by crediting as gospel the justly (and sometimes unjustly) proud breeders as they describe their wares. Do not buy a lethargic, shy, erratic dog that the breeder says "only acts like this at dog shows."

Look for dogs whose appearance might frighten you—there is good likelihood that they would also frighten others.

The giant breeds are occasionally subject to serious skeletal defects. Hip dysplasia is an abnormality of the large weight-supporting hip joint that may cause limping and serious gait problems. This problem is frequently found in these giant breeds. It is wise to obtain proof of the absence of this problem in the parents of the dog you are purchasing. The orthopedic foundation for animals (OFA) provides a classification system for hip x-rays taken when a dog is two years old. Although a pup cannot be certified by knowing the status of his parents, it is helpful in understanding the x-ray to evaluate the possibility that your pup will develop this problem as he grows to his adult size.

For those of us who would like to own a large purebred dog, and can afford both the food and cleanup difficulties, the heavyweights such as the Great Dane, Mastiff, St. Bernard and their brethren are worth considering. It is a good bet you will get a loud, intimidating, but 'gentle giant.'

A final word of caution: Do not buy a 'gentle giant' puppy if one of his parents acts overly aggressive or uncontrollable. Some of the giant breeds have poor reputations because of uncontrollable aggression and instability that has been produced by careless or ignorant breeding practices. Because of their size these breeds have the potential to easily overpower an adult human. It is best to realize that the very size of these dogs makes it mandatory that they be carefully trained in basic obedience exercises. Incorrect training or lack of training can lead to the dog's aggression toward the owner. Obviously, these dogs can become more dangerous to the owner and thus eliminate any value as companion or protector. We once received an hysterical call from a hospitalized dog owner whose untrained "vicious" Giant physically dragged her around the house for a terrifying fifteen minutes after an unprovoked attack. The owner said that she believed she would be killed when the huge dog repeatedly bit her and shook her as if she were a toy. This certainly is a dramatic exception to the usual stable and often docile behavior of the giant breeds, but their very potential for dominating is so great that they should never be looked upon as clowns or giant stuffed teddy bears.

The Real Thing

The "real thing" is a biting dog! He does not bluff—he attacks! There is no room for error, or false confidence when purchasing, training, owning or housing this animal.

Where to purchase "the real thing" is a major challenge—a challenge that should not be entertained without serious considerations of all of its aspects. The "attack dog" is a potential lethal weapon—one that can cripple, maim, disfigure, and cause big league mayhem, misery, and death. It follows that a decision to buy "the real thing" can be thought comparable to setting up a live booby trap in your home. It is a decision which can expose you to a lawsuit, criminal charges and, worst of all, the guilt of having been involved in a tragic accident that could have been avoided. But despite these monumental liabilities in possessing "the real thing"—a man-stopper—a tiny percentage of our population is at sufficient risk for life and limb to rationally make the decision to own this type of animal. After this decision is reached, locating "the real thing" can be as elusive as finding an exceptional, quality bargain in a used car lot. The difficulty can be best understood by the fact that the average potential purchaser of "the real thing" has less knowledge of his subject than the first-time car buyer on a used car lot. How can we then overcome our ignorance and naivete so as not to be cheated, hoodwinked and gulled into buying a 'garbage' animal at an extraordinary price? You will find the market place for selling guard dogs filled with hucksters, flim-flam men, and just plain old country boys—all trying to make some money selling you a dog.

Where to Buy Your Dog

If you have absolutely no knowledge about the breeds you should be considering, or no acquaintances with others who have purchased this type animal, then you must let your fingers do the walking through the commercial section of the telephone book under DOGS. There you will find the obligatory pictures of snarling dogs. Start with these telephone numbers. Many of these firms specialize in furnishing protection for retail outlets providing both human and canine guard service. Other firms specialize in training animals for protection. Either of these groups may be able to provide a suitable dog, but again—BUYER BEWARE. You must have in mind a series of screening questions for your initial inquiry. These questions must include:

1. What breeds of dogs are you selling?
2. What age is the dog?
3. Has the dog been sexually altered (spayed or castrated)?
4. Did you breed the dog, and do you own either or both of his parents?
5. Do you have a health record of shots (rabies, virus)?

The above questions are to define the basic health of the dog and get a sense of the seller's familiarity with the specific breed and the individual dog he is selling. If the seller does not know the complete answers to the above questions, call another number. It is important to have questions answered about the second phase—the quality of his services—before we visit his kennel or place of business. These questions should include:

1. How long have you been in this business?

DO NOT buy from a comparative newcomer unless you have excellent character/business references. It is characteristic for "guard dog" businesses to open and subsequently to discontinue operation within one or two years, leaving breached contracts and lawsuits. Some establishments will claim to be associated with a long-time established organization. Check it out. Frequently the open-close pattern is the same.

2. Do you provide a guarantee and trial period which would permit me to return the dog?
3. Will you provide after-the-sale training, and what will be the additional charge?
4. Have you competed in any type of dog sports such as obedience trials, tracking tests, or the German sport of Schutzhund or other protection dog sports?

As in many enterprises, the cream of the crop are proud of their accomplishments. Give the seller a chance to expound on what he has personally done as a dog trainer. If he denies or diminishes the importance of any recognized competition, bid him, "Adieu."

By now you have decided to visit your friendly protective dog dealer. What should you look for?

What is the physical layout of his place of business? Sleazy, shoddy, transient operations usually can be quickly recognized. Sometimes, if there are enough animals, a good inhalation through the nose is all that is needed. If it doesn't look right, leave. You are not going to find a gem hidden among dog feces, debris, and irregular swatches of chicken wire, field fences, or rusted chain link fence. The best vendor is probably a commercial kennel specializing in guard dog sales. A clean, modern kennel is very expensive to build as well as to operate. Therefore the kennel owner must plan for the future, and a good reputation is the only way he can stay in business.

If you are still interested after your initial survey, then walk directly to the business office and ask to speak with whomever you have previously discussed your requirements. Look around for pictures of the proprietor with his dogs. Signs of merit such as plaques, trophies, ribbons, and pictures of his "best" dogs will be available, either on the wall or stored nearby—unless he doesn't have any.

Briefly try to confirm your telephone conversation. Most of the dealers will be more open when you have shown commitment enough to make an appearance. At this time, however, he should not show any signs of backing away from his firm commitment to the quality of his animals **IN WRITING**. Ask for a demonstration. What should you expect to see:

1. The dog should be brought out of a clean place of habitation.

2. The dog should not be excessively thin or frightened. He should not be noisy in the company of his handler unless faced with the staged aggressor (in dog training circles called an agitator or helper). If only you and the handler are present the dog may bark once or twice but should not appear to be uncontrollably noisy or aggressive, but rather aloof and calm. A playful dog can be an excellent home protector so do not rule him out at first glance.

3. The demonstration should include off-leash obedience control. A dog that bolts from the handler and does not respond to commands is not having a bad day, he is a bad (disobedient) dog.

4. When faced with an aggressor, the dog should appear immediately alert, enthusiastic, and should become increasingly hostile by loud barking at the aggressor's approach. When released, the dog should directly seek to confront, seize, and do battle with this aggressor. The aggressor will be dressed in protective clothing that will include a padded sleeve. The real thing, in contrast to a sport dog, will bite when there is no visible sleeve. It will be only the agitators ability

61

"The Real Thing" (muzzled) on the way to attack.

to present an arm actually encased in a well padded sleeve that prevents the dog from biting another part of his anatomy. Most impressive is the dog's direct attack on the described sleeve, which is usually covered with a loose fitting jacket or overcoat.

5. ATTENTION! The dog must be able to be "called off" from the attack by **verbal** command. In this controlled situation, if the attack cannot be halted easily by the trainer's command without his resorting to physical contact in pulling off the dog, then you must assume the telephone repairman who comes through your back door doesn't stand a chance.

6. Don't be disappointed if the dog appears friendly and is easily handled. Often dogs that are kept for a period of time in a kennel become very docile. This dog will probably become very territorial and be an excellent protector within a few weeks. If the dog doesn't work out as promised then the seller will accept return of the dog as agreed in the sale contract. I remember a dog we sold that was a large well-trained, docile German Shepherd male. The buyer was very worried that the dog would not protect as we had guaranteed. It took almost six weeks, but the dog finally became impressively aggressive.

PURCHASE: The dog that you purchase should, under your direct observation, perform as well as the dog that has been demonstrated to you earlier. The dog you buy should be between twelve months and six years old. If the dog is four years old, because of the declining number of useful years in his protective occupation, there should be appropriate discount on the price you are asked to pay. A reasonable service life for the protection dog is eight to twelve years. If you are looking for the absolute extreme, such as a "man stopper," a male is usually superior. In circumstances requiring "the real thing" it might be better to hire a paramilitary group equipped with appropriate artillery for even more security. When children are present in the household, a female is the better choice. Neutered animals can be very effective home protectors. Neutering does not alter the protective ability of the bitch and a neutered male is not seriously limited in his protection role. His energy level and ability to be an all out manstopper seeking to dominate all he sees is likely to be diminished, but this does not necessarily lessen his performance in carrying out his general guarding duties. We call your attention to the fact that, despite the symbolic impression that the testicles are the source of all courage and strength, harem guards were eunuchs.

If you have bought "the real thing," you will do well to find an experienced trainer for your dog's maintenance. You can not buy a "man stopper" and then relax and forget it. Good luck!

"The Real Thing." This very serious imported German Shepherd tries to "kill" the bad guy—without a muzzle he would!

Great Pyrenees. This former Protector of flocks is now happy to guard suburban and country homes.

Rottweiler. Considered by some as "best" protection dog. However, the individual dog must be evaluated.

This Shih Tzu looks decorative but also is a great "sound alert" dog.

Breeds of Dogs

The first decision a prospective dog owner needs to make is, "what is the right breed for me?" This decision is very difficult when we look objectively at the various breeds. An objective search is often frustrated by well-meaning friends. If they are dog owners, they have already made their choice and are certain which breed is best!

When inquiring for information about the various breeds, you will encounter a forest of myths and overly complimentary descriptions of the breeds. Dog owners adjudge something exceptional about their breed and often perceive something that is a little bit wrong with the choice you were thinking about—if it is not the same as theirs.

You must realize that a decision cannot be based upon the intrinsic superiority of any breed of dog. Your own personal needs with regard to the dog's size, use, energy level, and grooming requirement are the true issues you must consider. These considerations are just a start toward a decision that will determine which breed you choose. Additionally there is also the emotional attraction that a specific breed of dog has for you. It is almost impossible to ignore your feeling that "this is the kind of dog I have always wanted."

In training protective dogs for more than twenty years, it has become clear that the old saying, "There are greater differences within the same breed of dog than there are between breeds," is true. To illustrate this we frequently have to explain to very disappointed owners that the meek and nervous animal they purchased was not guaranteed by the breeder to be a strong protective dog just because it was a Doberman Pinscher, Rottweiler, Giant Schnauzer, Bouvier Des Flandres, or German Shepherd. Moreover, these people are even more upset when they find their friends own a breed not known specifically for protection such as an Irish Setter, Labrador, or Dalmatian, and have an animal that is just what they would have wanted. These examples mean that there are wonderful candidates for protective companions in all breeds, and that the diversity of individuals within that breed is so wide that choice must be made on something more than breed name.

Perhaps this was not always so. Dogs that were originally bred for specific work, whether police, herding, or guard duty, were of similar temperament. But many years have passed since these breeds were originated and their popularity and numbers have expanded. Choices are now made for selecting breeding stock based upon reasons quite different from those that were used to create the breed. The utility type dogs are now chosen frequently for their gait, color, coat length, head structure, and color of the eye. Though these characteristics may make a pleasing picture they do not guarantee the qualities of a protective companion. For this reason, careful attention should be paid to the chapter on puppy testing.

With this disclaimer now imparted, there are general tendencies among breeds that may make one preferable to another for use as a home protector. Dogs listed as working or herding dogs frequently do make the best home protectors whether they are trained to be true biting dogs or to only show signs of visual intimidation. An interesting example of the balance between breed and environment is a case in which a protection-bred German Shepherd male was raised with a litter of Beagles. When he was one year old the Shepherd would hunt just as well as the beagles, and showed little behavioral resemblance to the protective animal he had been bred to become.

In the advertising pages of dog magazines there are listed an abundance of breeds, kennels, and breeders. These ads portray the merits of their particular dogs as companions and potentially protective animals. This glut of advertising is confusing and sometimes quite misleading. In order to make an informed judgement, there is some benefit in categorizing breeds of dogs to outline a framework in which to make a better "guesstimate."

The Real Thing

Dogs that are candidates for being the "Real Thing" are potentially serious guard animals which are capable of doing great bodily harm when commanded or when they perceive a threat to their human family or territory. In other circumstances they can be deceivingly friendly or show only an aloof disposition. These dogs have had aggressive tendencies honed, and strengthened by professional training. The real thing may be compared to a commando, or member of a SWAT team trained to do injury under orders. He is not to be confused with a homicidal maniac or his canine equivalent, the vicious dog.

Newspaper accounts of children being injured by dogs rarely involve what we call the "real thing." These tragic accounts most likely relate to an untrained animal that pursues the child as he would chase game. Many fighting dogs recently have been implicated in child injury cases. It is not clear whether there is a genetic relationship between selectively bred fighting dogs and the apparent child aggression they exhibit. These dogs usually have not had protection training and often surprise their owner with unexpected aggression. We have had great difficulty in developing a controlled protective response in these animals that have shown unpredictable aggression.The real thing is **not erratic** and can be expected to behave in a predictable manner with aggression if challenged or if his territory is invaded. Fighting breeds generally are unsuitable for family protection as their ownership requires constant supervision. They are more practical as a "professional" protector such as a police service dog.

One breed can have specimens that fall into all categories of protective dogs. Some breeds however, produce higher percentages of the type that you consider suitable. The following breed descriptions are based upon the types of dogs within a breed and the general popularity of that breed. These factors should influence your choice of the dog you buy.

Common Dogs

The common of breeds of dogs, of which there may be more than fifty thousand new individual registrations each year, have the advantage of being readily accessible. In these breeds there is often a lower initial price and one has tremendous opportunity to shop around among various breeders. The liability of these common dogs is that their very numbers also provide hundreds of thousands of potentially inferior, unsuitable products of uninformed breeding. It is members of these breeds that are most commonly handled by commercial breeders, sold in pet stores, and often have multiple genetic problems—from bony deformities to bleeding disorders. With these breeds meticulous research, careful cross-checking of references, and personal examination of the parents of any pup is essential if you are to make an intelligent decision. The German Shepherd, Doberman Pinscher, and Rottweiler are examples of these popular breeds.

The Great Dane. Imposing "gentle giant."

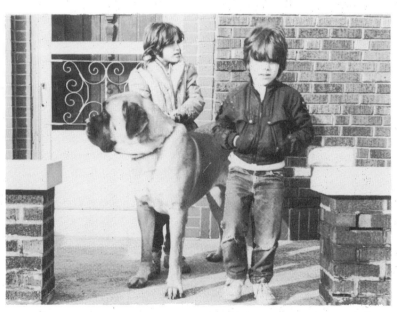

Old English Mastiff. This gentle giant lives in the city and is an "apartment" dog.

Increasingly Popular Dogs

If you study the breed registries of the American Kennel Club over the last twenty-five years it is evident that there are cyclic fads in breeds. The course of these fads includes a growth phase, a logarithmic increase in growth of the breed's population, a leveling-off of the population, and finally a decline. During the rapid increase of growth some terrible problems may arise. They come from the profit incentives that cause more dogs to be produced for an increasing market. Breeding selectivity changes and while the number of puppies produced that are of exceptional quality may increase, the relative percentage decreases dramatically. This is a paradox—the original reason for the increasing popularity may have been the exceptional individuals in the show ring or the obedience ring. The reputation of these individuals generates enthusiasm for the breed and demand increases. Thus, what was valuable and extraordinary can (and does) become diluted and distorted.

With this warning expressed, the following breeds are often of excellent quality but their increasing popularity must make one careful that they have not chosen an animal indiscriminately bred from a "puppy mill."

These protection dogs generally weigh 60 to 100 pounds, are potentially aggressive, and with the exception of the American Staffordshire Terrier, they are classified in the working or herding groups of dogs. They include such breeds as the Bouvier des Flandres, American Staffordshire Terrier, Giant Schnauzer, Akita, and Bull Mastiff.

Uncommon Dogs

This group of dogs can provide some of the most interesting and exciting choices when you are looking for that special dog. The dogs listed below are in most cases quite rare, and a number of them have not yet been recognized by the American Kennel Club. They are all purebred dogs recognized either by the AKC or other kennel clubs of the world. Their place of origin ranges from the steppes of Asia Minor, as the Akbash dog and the Anatolian Shepherd, to the plains of Hungary, as the Kuvasz.

These are large dogs—some used for hunting Jaguar and men, as the Fila Brasileiro from the pampas and jungles of South America. Pioneering spirit is required, when looking for these animals, yet an incredibly rich lore is usually available from Americans that have imported these dogs. Importers and breeders of rare breeds are usually

Belgian Malinois are becoming more popular with police departments because of their agility and intelligence.

Imported Malinois on the attack.

exceedingly enthusiastic and enjoy discussing with a potential buyer the history and qualities of their dogs. They are often exuberant in describing their new-found rare breed and can provide rich stories of how they became interested in their particular dog.

One of the inherent advantages of rare breeds, as well as those of quite limited popularity, is that the breeding programs of these breeds have not yet been subjected to fads or indiscriminate breeding. Dogs of these relatively uncommon breeds are often only several generations removed from their working predecessors. Some of the rare breeds are currently utilized in the United States in research testing programs directed toward obtaining superior ranch and farm guard dogs. These dogs, imported from Asia and central Europe, are being employed in the western United States to protect sheep and cattle from predators. The Akbash dog, Anatolian Shepherd, Great Pyrenees and Kuvasz are four breeds that are being evaluated in this research project.

The potential limitations of these rare breeds also must be considered. The imported dogs are often from parents, who unlike most American utility breeds, have not been subjected to x-ray clearance of hip disease. This problem, which troubles most large dogs to a varying degree, is not being screened by the more remote rural and farm communities from which they arise. The frequency of genetic abnormalities, including hip dysplasia, is poorly documented. Additionally, as the rare dogs generate some interest, we, unfortunately, will encounter the sellers of mixed breed dogs represented as rare breeds. We recall one such salesman of the very rare "Alaskan Alsatian." He said this very extraordinary uncommon dog was bred by eskimos to protect sled dogs and humans from wild predators—obviously an exceedingly expensive, very rare breed. Actually there is no such breed registered anywhere. In fact, the dog in question was actually a large, long-coated German Shepherd who was registered with the AKC. To prevent such misrepresentation from succeeding, know your subject. Careful investigation is required of the person who is selling these dogs. Official documentation of the pedigree and confirmed knowledge of the length of time the breeder or seller has been associated with the rare breed is bound to be helpful.

There is a variety of the Belgian Sheepdog, which is actually a subset of the Belgian Malinois, known as the KNPV dog. KNPV is a training organization, not a breed of dog. These dogs are bred in Holland primarily for police work. As working dogs they often have a somewhat different appearance (conformation) than the standard Malinois which itself is a rare AKC breed. Our experience with the

KNPV titled dogs is excellent. The police breeding programs from which they are derived have created a relatively homogenous group of outgoing, athletic, and stable animals which shows a great deal of enthusiasm in training. Similar dogs are often successful competitors in what is described in Europe as the "ring sports." This advanced form of dog sport/protection competition, is similar to that of Schutzhund but in some ways more demanding. The animal in this sport faces an agile, well protected human assailant, who fends off the dog in a much more energetic manner than the more stylized Schutzhund-agitator role. The Belgian Malinois and particularly the KNPV dogs, have been exceedingly successful in all forms of protection competition. Though in some eyes he appears to be a small, tan, German Shepherd, in fact he is a distinct breed unto himself. Yet there is no breed registry for the KNPV dog!

The Beauceron, is a long-haired shepherd-type dog bred primarily in France. This breed shares some physical characteristics which appear to be almost a hybrid between that of the Doberman Pinscher and the German Shepherd.

The Tosa is a dog imported from Japan, where it was developed as a large (greater than 90 pounds) fighting dog. It was developed over the last fifty years by cross-breeding with imports from Europe, including Mastiff and Great Dane, and combining these with indigenous dogs of Japan.

The dogs listed below provide the reader with a general survey of the rare and unusual breeds that may be both interesting and desirable to bring into your home as a potential protective dog. We suggest that these dogs be purchased as puppies and also recommend, as with other puppy purchases, that you insist on a replacement contract in case there are significant health problems associated with the puppy's development. These breeds are: Anatolian Shepherd, Beauceron, Dogue of Bordeaux, Fila Brasileiro, Komondor, Kuvasz, Belgian Sheepdog (Tervuren, Malinois, Groenendael, and KNPV), Akbash Dog and Tosa.

Breeds Suitable as Gentle Giants

The dogs listed below share one major attribute. It is their great size. These dogs often are derived from what are called the Mollosus breeds, which were the forefathers of the Mastiff type animals. They are usually greater than one hundred pounds and, in examples of the

72

St. Bernard, Mastiff, and Tibetan Mastiff, approach two hundred pounds. A few breeds, including the Tibetan Mastiff, Neapolitan Mastiff, and Great Pyrenees, run the gauntlet of being not only Gentle Giants but capable of a much more animated role. The Neapolitan Mastiff is rapidly increasing in numbers and distribution. This once exceedingly rare dog is now being bred more extensively in the United States and being sold as an aggressive home watch dog. Because of his size we have serious concerns that exploitative breeding combined with the promotion of the breed as an aggressive animal may create serious problems. These problems can occur with **any** very large breed. An aggressive, two hundred pound animal should be in a zoo and not in your home. We have seen enormous strength exhibited by a 'Gentle Giant' who pulled a fence out of the ground which had been secured with railroad ties! In a second circumstance another 'Gentle Giant' pulled his owner off her feet and dragged her more than one hundred feet down a concrete sidewalk as he chased another dog.

It is important when dealing with these massive breeds to obtain information from the breeder about the character and temperament qualities of the parents. We recommend direct observation of the parents if at all possible. The examples above are the exceptions to the way these large animals usually behave. Properly bred, with attention to temperament and careful training from a young age, they can be wonderful home companions.

A biological fact: a dog's normal lifespan is usually inversely related to its size. The giant breeds live relatively short lives.

The large dogs are capable of baying a rather intimidating alarm. They are often less sensitive to the presence of children in the home and are frequently difficult to "stir up." In the same light, however, the basso profunda barking of these animals should be taken to represent a true alarm. They are not likely to be easily provoked and can serve quite well, in the presence of adequate space, as a visual deterrent and high threshold alarm system. These dogs include Saint Bernard, Great Dane, Briard, Mastiff, Alaskan Malamute, Newfoundland, Neapolitan Mastiff, Bernese Mountain Dog, Tibetan Mastiff, Great Pyrenees, and Irish Wolfhound.

The Sound Alert Dogs

The sound alert dogs provide low threshold alarm. They are easily triggered into barking and frenetic activity. Their yips, barks, and high level activity—investigating every nook and cranny of a house or an apartment—make them fine animated intruder alerts. They are typically small, usually less that 40 pounds, long-lived, and maintain a youthful, high-spirited existence well into their later years. They behave as if they are unaware how small they are and are quite willing to present themselves as a deterrent to an intruder. Obviously their small size generally limits them to auditory deterrence.

Two breeds, the Kerry Blue and Airedale Terrier, do make the transition to physical protection and are capable of engaging in serious physical deterrents. These two breeds can be exceedingly aggressive, territorial, and if not well trained, the males of these breeds are capable of biting their owners, fighting other dogs, and asserting their will in the household.

The terrier-type sound alert dogs were originally bred to "go to ground." They were used to hunt and seize burrowing animals and were therefore bred as an aggressive, tenacious bundle of animal energy often encased in a very small compact package. They are not to be trifled with and are less forgiving with children as far as tolerating abuse.

In the proper family setting any one of the Terrier breeds listed below would fulfill the classic description of an animated alarm system: Fox Terrier, Cairn Terrier, Irish Terrier, Dandie Dinmont Terrier, Kerry Blue Terrier, Airedale, Scottish Terrier, Sealyham Terrier, Skye Terrier, and Wheaten Terrier.

Non-Terrier Sound Alert Dogs

The animals listed below have the characteristics of exhibiting high energy but are larger animals than most Terriers. They are not known for obvious aggressive or territorial behavior but can give a barking alarm or present a visually intimidating appearance. Their hunting background has created an exceedingly high energy animal requiring significant exercise. They do tend to be less territorial than the working and utility dogs and less sedate than the dogs listed as Gentle Giants. For some individuals, these dogs may supply utility both as a home alarm and companion. These breeds include the Beagle, Weimaraner, Pointers (German Shorthaired, German Wirehaired), Vizsla, Retrievers (Chesapeake Bay, Labrador). The one non-sporting member belonging with the above group is the Welsh Corgi. Though he properly falls in the herding dog list, his small size precludes him from being a true physical deterrent. The Welsh Corgi, however, can be strongly territorial, vocal and quite willing to administer a strong bite below the waist.

Two interesting animals that are still quite rare and not listed by the American Kennel Club but are purebred dogs are the Glen of Imaal and German Hunting Terrier. Both of these breeds—the former imported from Ireland, the latter from Germany—are feisty, vocal, and, in the case of the German Hunting Terrier, possibly the pocket version of the Real Thing.

Small Sound Alert Dogs

These are the micro-canine alarm systems. These yippie, animated and territorial animals are quite excellent for those that want to deal with an animal of less than twenty-five pounds. The breeders of these small animals are frequently "hobby breeders" and will truly try to provide a good companion. These small breeds are not, however, generally optimal for those who have rambunctious children, as both injury to the dog and to the child can happen in a quite unexpected manner. Yippie dogs do nip and this can sometimes be of greater hazard to the owner than to any potential intruder. With this caveat the small sound alert dog can provide hours of pleasurable companionship as well as keeping a watchful eye and sharp bark ready for anyone who might intrude. These breeds include the Pomeranian, Affenpinscher, Yorkshire Terrier, Australian Terrier, Pekingese, Pug, Miniature Spitz, Miniature Poodle, and Schipperke.

The last of these dogs listed—the Schipperke—is of particular interest. He is an exceedingly long-lived black dog who was actually derived from larger herding types and is said to have been bred to be a boatman's dog. He served during the last century as a watch dog for those that kept their wares and homes on the water in Europe. In our experience we have found that he is an excellent sound alert animal.

Retrieving can be tested by getting the puppy's attention on a ball.

Natural retrieving inclination is an advantage in a training prospect.

Pup should be interested when beckoned—even better if he will walk over obstruction.

Relaxed and calm—ideal response for pup picked up by scruff of neck.

Puppy Testing

Take your time in choosing a puppy. The decision may affect your life for many years to come. The size of the dog or the texture of his coat is far less important than the way he learns. Protective dogs will demonstrate temperament in a consistent fashion through many generations when breeding is planned with consistent behavior as the prime goal. Look long and well at the mother, father, sister, brother, aunt, uncle and grandparents of the puppies. The inherited temperament can make the task of turning this cuddly ball of fur into the companion you want either easy or impossible.

If you are inexperienced selecting a puppy can be significantly helped by employing a series of tests. These tests, though not absolute, give insight into the character that the puppy will be likely to develop. It will be impossible to select a puppy while listening to a sales pitch, and simultaneously trying to separate a mass of squirming young puppies. To bring some order into this confusion we have provided a series of observations and maneuvers that should help.

There are many tests available. Unfortunately many of them require an experienced examiner to evaluate the results. We have taken the test process we felt was best and adapted it for the general reader. A single object, a plastic quart soda bottle filled with small pebbles, is the only piece of equipment required. These tests, done in the order that is described, should greatly assist the potential buyer. It is useful to be accompanied by another person, so that notes may be taken and the observations discussed by two individuals from different vantage points.

This analysis is an attempt to evaluate the confidence, human bonding, trainability, and dominance of a particular animal. These general qualities can be tested during one evaluation, although additional sessions would be helpful.

Please keep in mind that the types of animals that we have described—the sound alert dog, the gentle giant, the real thing, and a non-protective companion dog—will exhibit varying mixtures of the following traits. We have already outlined ways to select breeders, as

77

well as other sources for dogs. When at a breeder's home the puppy should be examined in comparison with his littermates. Optimally one, or preferably both, parents should be observed. And, if individuals of previous similar breedings are available for observation, all the better!

Testing

The ideal time to test temperament is at six to nine weeks of age, or as soon as the motor skills are developed. If the opportunity is available then retesting weekly at least twice would be optimal.

Puppy testing is performed as a series of observations of games and maneuvers, with the young dogs. Between the ages of six to nine weeks the puppy exhibits basic natural tendencies and character traits. He is old enough to begin acting in response to his environment, yet not so mature that he has been significantly modified by human or canine interaction and training. We employ staged games and maneuvers for choosing a puppy who will grow to suit our needs. The "real thing" potential puppy will test differently than the "sound alert" dog.

These tests are used to determine the puppy's inherent compatibility with our needs. We will be examining his acceptance of strangers, confidence, protectiveness, trainability, innate dominance, and energy levels.

Approaching

The approach to a litter of puppies between six and nine weeks old can be the first puppy test. No equipment is necessary in this first step of your evaluation—only an observant attitude. In a planned way, you as a stranger to these young dogs, will look at them, pick them up, place them down, startle them, and restrain them. Their reactions to these maneuvers should be recorded. Often it is best if a friend comes with a notebook, or video tape, to record these previously discussed and rehearsed maneuvers.

Following is a series of simple steps which can be taken on a one-day visit to the breeder.

1)   Walk to the litter enclosed in a pen. Approach the fence and stand without speaking for thirty seconds, making eye contact with the puppies. The following reactions are likely:

a) One or more of the puppies will surge forward to investigate.

b) One or more will retreat and possibly vocalize by barking or growling or whining.

c) One or more will stand his ground and vocalize by barking, whining, or growling.

d) One or more will continue as if you never approached, totally ignoring your presence.

Interpretation:

a) Most of us tend to favor the puppy that investigates us. The vast majority of people will pick the puppy which most exuberantly acknowledges our presence. This is a very good choice for a family home companion. He may have the potential to become a protective dog, and should be considered as a candidate worthy of further testing.

b) This puppy is the exact opposite to the one chosen in "a." He is suspicious, and not confident. This is the least desirable animal for those seeking a safe home companion. When mature this animal may respond fearfully (the classic "fear biter") to sudden actions by neighbors or childhood friends with snaps and bites in an effort to protect himself. This is, however, a dog that can be employed as a sound alert animal. He will reliably vocalize (warn) at the approach of strangers. An unfamiliar young child or hooded gunman are all the same to this walking alarm system. These qualities in a miniature or toy breed are often acceptable and almost humorous, but would be dangerous in the large and giant breeds. We feel all giants should be gentle. A dog that can easily reach your face and engulf your head in his jaws can't afford to make a neurotic mistake. In the utility breeds such as German Shepherds, Rottweilers, Dobermans, Bouviers, or Giant Schnauzers this temperament is a poor choice in all circumstances.

c) This puppy is a very interesting choice. His lack of confidence is in a balanced state. He may overcome his fear through greater aggressive displays and could mature into a dangerous animal. He is a variant of the "fear biter" who protects himself by attempting to dominate those who would challenge him. His confidence is attained through defensive aggression. The fear in this young dog will never be seen as an adult if he succeeds during his growth to frighten first those who frighten him. Aggressive displays will be used by this dog in order to reduce his own fear of his environment.

d) This puppy is the least likely to evoke our interest unless we seek a "pet rock" that requires feeding and cleaning. For whatever reason we do not make an impression on him, and his future is one where human beings are of little value or interest. This dog will be low drive, low activity and therefore very easy to live with. He may develop into a sound alert protector.

The next portion of our testing requires the puppy that we have decided is of interest to us based on the previous testing to be taken away from the litter. It is important that the puppy be removed from sight and sound of his littermates and taken to a strange place where we may examine him. Much valuable information can be obtained by closely watching his response to being picked up and carried as he is brought to us.

Cradling

Pick up the puppy and cradle him in your arms as you would a baby. Scratch his chest and talk to him in a soothing tone, look toward him but do not stare, tilt your head in a submissive way.

1) The puppy should look at you and completely relax in your arms to the extent that he feels heavy. He should mold to your body and look into your eyes, not past you. It is not unusual for the ideal competitive training prospect to accept this position only for a short time. When he attempts to break loose observe whether he turns towards you or away from you. It is hoped he will turn toward you. The companion dog will have a lower drive than the protection prospect and will remain in the cradling position indefinitely. All these responses are considered ideal.

2) It is less desirable if the puppy turns his head away—demonstrating a lack of confidence. The insecure puppy will show the whites of his eyes. If you hold him firmly until he stops struggling he will learn to tolerate cradling. The struggling is a result of fear. The puppy that is slow to tolerate cradling may appear to be quite independent but is fearful. This dog at maturity will require a firm hand with compulsive training.

3) The puppy progresses as in #1. He rolls toward the handler and stops half-way (feet facing the handler). First he will look at the handler and then to his surroundings. We misunderstood this behavior when we first began testing. Experience has shown that this puppy will be very difficult to live with and train.

4) The puppy screams, cries, fights, maybe urinates. This is an unacceptable response.

The companion dog puppy should be milder and more responsive to cradling—almost melting in your arms. Both companion and high energy puppies may do a lot of licking. The poor prospect will panic, remain stiff and motionless in your arms. He may cry or soil you while he is held.

Farmer's Test

Grasp the puppy by the loose skin on the top of his neck, behind his ears and above the point of his shoulders (the withers). Massage his neck gently and then maintain your grip and lift the puppy off the floor, smoothly and gently.

1) The best response is for the puppy to be relaxed and silent. You may even notice the puppy feeling very heavy, like a dead weight. His feet should hang limply, muzzle pointing downward.

2) The puppy's muzzle points up or out, his toes spread, his legs stiffen. As you suspend the puppy his legs draw upward with the toes spread. This is a tolerable reaction but not ideal.

3) As in #2 but the puppy becomes vocal. This response is unacceptable.

4) As in #2 and #3 but the puppy urinates and/or defecates, may even try to bite. This response is totally unacceptable.

This test is designed to measure stability, security and confidence. If you only had time to perform one test this would be the best choice. This is why it has been named "the farmer's test." A natural explanation of the value of this test can be seen with a litter that is threatened by a fire. The mother picks up the puppies one at a time and moves them to safety. If the puppy fought and struggled it would not survive.

Pinning

The next exercise is known as "pinning." We do not wrestle the puppy to the ground. Firmly and gently place one hand on the puppy's neck below his ears and above the point of his shoulders (withers). Massage his neck gently to obtain a handful of loose skin while placing the other hand above his flank along his spine (the beginning of his croup). Pull the puppy to the floor on his side and hold him in this position for approximately three to five seconds. The tester is not to assert his dominance but to remain neutral and benevolent.

Reactions:

1) The puppy lies relaxed and silent, offering no resistance while being held. His head should be on the floor with his legs relaxed. This is the most desirable reaction. This puppy is adaptable and has the ability to adjust to new situations. This dog may be dominant or he may not, this particular test is not designed to make this determination.

2) The puppy writhes, bites, growls, fights, and does not cease struggling until you release your grip.

This is not an acceptable response. This puppy shows an inclination toward handler (owner) aggression. This dog is difficult to train, more headstrong, and will require compulsive training effort—something most owners are not willing to do. As this puppy matures he will challenge household members, children, old folks alike. Even if you are a firm, dominant trainer, you must consider the other family members who will live with your dog.

3) The puppy struggles as in #2, then becomes calm. Also an unacceptable response. This puppy has desire to dominate yet will accept the reality of greater force, and is more trainable than the dog in #2.

4) The puppy that hysterically fights for life, often loosing control of bladder and bowels. This is the most undesirable reaction. This puppy will be frustrating and stubborn to train. Fear again is his most manifest character trait.

The above "pinning" test tells a great deal about the adaptability of your future companion. Cooperation without fear provides the most capable canine student. Inflexibility, obstinacy, and fear inhibit learning. Training the obstinate, unadaptable dog results in an annoyed and unhappy dog with a very frustrated trainer. In a formal obedience competition this dog would be very disappointing. Fear interrupts the learning process and substitutes a flight response.

The pinning test will assist us in determining the likelihood of a dog being able to turn the tables on us in the learning process. The inflexible dog is threatened by everyone in his environment, and therefore must control to avoid experiencing his fear. This canine reaction appears to be dominance but requires different handling than the truly dominant dog. The responses described in#2, #3, and #4 are found in animals who have successfully trained their owners. In other words these dogs have taught their owners not to bother them while they are eating, not groom or bathe them, allow them to be aggressive toward other dogs, and accompany them where THEY want to go even if it is through mud, snow, or busy streets.

Following

The second maneuver with this same puppy is to observe his behavior as you back away from him, beckoning, and stopping periodically.

1) The puppy immediately leaves you. This does not mean he does not love you. It may mean that he has found something more interesting, as confident and investigative puppies often do. Can you whistle, clap your hands or make sounds that get his attention? If not, does he run further away from these noises that you are making? If he runs further away he certainly is not reassured by human presence and displays lack of confidence of his new environment. We would rather see outgoing, confident behavior in which he at least stops and tries to figure out what these sounds are. The puppy may even return to you, exhibiting both curiosity and confidence. This is the optimal response.

2) The puppy stays with you, touching, clinging, or jumping on you and does not leave. The puppy that has to touch or cling is not acceptable. Although it appears that human beings are important to this puppy, it is for all the wrong reasons, even though bonding occurs easily. This puppy is in a strange environment and looks to you, the strange person, as a possible protector. This is not an acceptable response, and generally does not provide the best choice for a well-rounded protection dog.

Another possible response similar to the above 'clinger' is the puppy that follows the tester and stays near, but does not cling. Although the

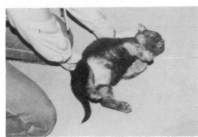

"Pinning" (holding down) shows much about temperament. This pup struggles to get free.

This pup demonstrates ideal response—calm and trusting.

puppy does stay in the immediate vicinity of the tester this puppy is lacking in confidence but is acceptable. This puppy will make a good companion dog but most likely will not be an optimal protection dog.

Sound Sensitivity

Before touching the puppy we must examine his reaction to sudden sights and sounds. A container, one gallon plastic milk bottle, or quart plastic soda bottle containing several small stones should be thrown within the puppy's vicinity (approximately twelve feet) forcefully enough to make considerable noise.
Reactions:

1) The puppy ignores or does not seem to respond to this sudden stimulus. This can be compared to an autistic child. the puppy is in his own world. Interaction with humans will be difficult and maybe impossible. In rare cases the dog may have sensory impairment such as deafness or visual defect.

2) The puppy startles at the sound and sight of the object and scurries away with no further interest. This puppy is not confident and will not adapt easily to new environments. Fear overrides other drives thus diminishing his ability to learn. No matter what our best intentions are we will not be able to provide him an enriched period of socialization and puppyhood.

3) The puppy startles, regains composure, and returns to investigate. This is a favorable response with both awareness of his environment and curiosity and confidence overcoming his initial fear.

4) No startled reaction followed by immediate investigation. This puppy has a level of confidence that is pronounced. This puppy is likely to be self-reliant, and is comfortable making decisions. And he will require an equally confident, knowledgeable trainer.

The above tests are the most basic, and can be performed by anyone. We advise thinking about them, having another person objectively write down the response in a notebook and then exchange observations about different puppies. This is the first step to an enlightened choice and is designed to avoid the heartbreak of choosing a puppy that really will not be able to become the dog you want.

We have discovered that temperaments fall into two general classifications—those based in fear and those based in confidence. The best way to avoid problems is to disqualify puppies whose dispositions are based in fear. All dogs can be trained but only the confident, adaptable, and stable prospect will mature into the ideal companion.

The tests will help sort out the potential prospect of companion dog, sound alert dog, and avoid potentially dangerous traits in what should be a gentle giant. The "real thing" can be approached from several different character configurations. More about this later.

The companion dog from the above tests should be trainable, non-dominant, bond rapidly to people, and does not need to be either investigative, energetic, or even exceedingly confident. We have found that, for this animal, confidence and the inclination not to startle easily is best suited for those who will have children in proximity of the dog.

The sound alert dog often is best chosen from the less confident, easily startled, and vocal puppies.

The visually intimidating breeds are usually members of the working or herding breeds and can make a great show of defense. Some of their intimidation originates from their being members of the same breed that are identified as police or guard dogs. One should keep in mind that any medium size to large dog that bares his teeth and vocalizes is a deterrent.

When choosing a puppy it is best to keep in mind what one truly wants in the adult animal. The type of puppy that will grow to a real man-stopper will often have qualities that are different than an animal that is "all show and no go." Dog breeding is still an inexact science. We must carefully examine the individual puppy. It is a mistake to be swayed by legends or an inflated reputation of any breed but rather accept the work required to examine the specific puppy you are seeking to buy. This testing is best used within a larger plan which includes our intended use of a dog. Companion dog, intimidating dog, gentle giant, or sound alert dog will be more easily obtained by testing for those characteristics which will fit into our long range plans.

The "real thing" more than any of the other dogs is a product of both genetic potential and training. Depending upon training techniques, two quite different sets of characteristics can be instilled into a dog that will be a man-stopper. The non-confident but dominant type of animal can be taught to act aggressively so that with training, his lack of confidence is hidden and in many ways over-compensated. The other animal which we cherish when found is the happy, confident, and playfully aggressive dog. If these features are combined with a strong territorial drive less intense training is required to produce the home protector that is a pleasure to have in your household.

GENTLE GIANT

Housing

Often ignored by the new dog owner is where the dog will stay. We have asked new owners where they plan to keep their puppy and they answer, "In the house, of course!" Then they often say, "I also have a fenced yard." These answers may seem suitable but are really inadequate.

Housing your dog properly is a fundamental aspect of guiding his development and providing a form of training by controlling his environment. Training by housing is frequently overlooked even by more experienced trainers. What do we mean by housing? Housing is the confinement of the dog to a physical structure or area of property which permits the dog to sleep, rest, remove himself from the various environmental stimuli such as other dogs, people, noises, and sights to which he feels he must respond. The most advantageous housing can be accomplished in a crate (metal, plastic, or wood box) that most people are familiar with having seen this type of carrier used by airlines in transporting dogs.

The least advantageous housing is having a dog run loose within a yard containing no structure and forcing the dog to try to get out of the elements by seeking shelter under trees, in barns, garages or other outside auxiliary buildings. The impact of housing on the dog cannot be overemphasized. The same puppy trained by the same person will develop into a fundamentally different dog based upon his housing. His housing will determine his socialization or isolation.

What do we seek in the development of the appropriate housing? This question must be answered in two parts, depending on the age of the dog.

For the puppy we are seeking to provide shelter and confinement so that we may control his interaction with people to provide optimal learning. We will confine him during non-learning times so that he does not develop habit patterns such as destruction of property, undesirable barking, aggression toward children, acceptance of all strangers etc. In some ways this latter aspect can be thought of as over-socialization. This is indiscriminate exposure to everyone within his home. The over-socialized puppy might never find unusual or peculiar a midnight stranger prying open your back door. If everyone's a friend, why bark?

What is a dog crate and how do we use the crate? First of all a dog crate is a metal or plastic enclosure sized according to the particular weight and height of the breed. For example a crate used for a German Shepherd weighing about 80 pounds would be 26 inches high, by 40 inches long by 24 inches wide. The first and most fundamental use for the crate is for puppy housebreaking. Unless our future protective dog is only to be a yard dog, toilet manners will be needed as he shares our living space. Because a dog is a den animal, his confinement in a relatively small and enclosed space, such as a crate, is not a cruelty, but rather a replication of his natural desire to find a burrow or small cave for his home. It is interesting to observe the circling behavior of a dog before he lies down, as he duplicates the behavior of other den-dwelling animals fitting themselves into their home. We can take advantage of these natural instincts in training so as to make a happier and cleaner companion in our home. The dog "naturally" will not foul his den. Thus, unlike grazing animals (sheep, cattle, etc.), he must keep his residence clean because he cannot defecate and then depart! He must come back to his den.

GOOD HOUSING

We strongly recommend the simultaneous purchase of a crate large enough to house a full sized dog at the time of taking delivery of your puppy. From his first day in your home, the dog should be introduced to his crate. Despite whining, barking, scratching, do not let him out until he is quiet and you have a purpose such as letting him go outside to relieve himself. An observation that may be helpful in the first few days to determine if the dog needs to relieve himself or is only trying to get out of the crate is to watch for circling or spinning movement—the sign of a call to nature. Alternating with his time in the crate should be the directed plan and training program that we have described earlier. Thus, during his first several months, ninety percent or more of the time will be spent in his crate. NO! This is not cruel, not solitary confinement, not punishment—but a reproduction of the natural order of things for the puppy. The crate should not be in the basement, closet, garage, or any secluded place. One must accept that its appearance will change the overall decor of your home, but that is much more desirable than letting the unconfined puppy change the decor to suit himself—such as tearing down the drapes from blocking his vision of the outside world.

As the dog matures, and his housebreaking progresses, the crate will become more of a nighttime residence. During the daytime, if someone is home and can observe and correct the young dog, he may slowly have his territory expanded one room at a time. We have found that with the large utility and herding breeds it is foolish to give a dog who is less than one year old the run of the house. The transition from crate confinement and directed training outside of the crate to independent life in your home is gradual. Rushing the dog through this in order "to give him freedom" is forcing an unfair responsibility upon the young dog.

We should look back at our own child-rearing and ask why we expect more from a young dog than from a young child. It would be sheer lunacy to leave a two-year-old child unattended in your home all day. This would be irresponsible and dangerously negligent of the child's safety. Poisoning by cleaning compounds, electrocution by playing with wires and wall sockets, scalding, house fires and burnings, are too often the fate of the child without supervision. The puppy's level of activity and ability to chew open containers, chew through wires, and exposed electrical connections, is even greater than that of a child. We doubt it would be possible to find a sympathetic ear if your antique porcelain was broken after you had left your three-year old nephew alone in the house for nine hours. One must wonder about the mentality of people who seek to be "nice" to their dogs by leaving them to roam free at the age of six months, discover the dog has destroyed property and punish him several hours after the act because the dog "looked guilty" when they came home. We must wonder if they would beat their nephew or niece—whose understanding of what occurred is probably tenfold that of the young dog.

The security that the crate provides a young dog is very important to his development because we are in control of his activity, and we have provided a place which gives him respite from stress. The crate is his resting place—his safe haven—not a punishment. For the older dog who has the run of the house, one will often find him voluntarily returning to his crate for sleep or rest. Often when untoward events occur, such as thunder, he will return to this place of safety, just as the wild animal caught in a thunderstorm will seek to return to the comfort and safety of his den.

Housing for the adult dog is less a training technique, but more a method to position the dog so he will be placed for optimal use. The type of house and its location will dictate the space that can be provided for the dog. The type of dog also will determine what the security requirements for this space should be. The "real thing," "gentle giant," or "sound alert" dog each require different types of housing. If one has the "real thing," then restriction must be placed upon his freedom because any one entering your home could meet a full set of canine fangs during their attempted visit. This type of housing will likely be that which confines the dog from coming in contact with people during times we would expect visitors, workmen, or others with benign intentions, to arrive at your front door. When this dog has the run of your home, beware. He recognizes no casual visitors. For this reason, the small number of people who have learned to live with this animated wrecking machine usually have him confined during the day. He will be in a place from which, at a moment's notice, he may be released to freely patrol the home. We must again remind the owner of this dog that he may encounter a lawsuit. Thus, your financial stability may also depend upon his proper housing, which is a controlled confinement. A crate, kennel-run attached to the house, or even a utility or work room that is locked and does not permit casual entry, should be employed while the dog is not on duty.

In contrast to the "real thing," the "gentle giant's" housing is much easier to provide. This is a dog large enough to intimidate by his appearance and baritone bark. Thus, he should be visible from the outside of the house. This is a dog that can stand up and look out the window, bark in a serious manner from behind a screened or glass door, and then be put away when visitors enter so that his gentleness is not exposed. This dog may be compared to the plugged barrel, non-firing replica of a .45 Colt—it is hard to look down the barrel of that Colt to be sure it is **really NON-FIRING.** Your "gentle giant" may have the run of the house day and night. If the chance stranger walks in without canine opposition, good public relations dictate that you tell him it was lucky for him that you told the "gentle giant" he was "all right."

The "sound alert" dog can be thought of as a working pet. Unlike the real thing who has been trained to patrol, the sound alert dog's natural uneasiness of strangers will generally permit the most liberal housing. He will not normally become over-socialized. The suspicious sound alert dog will bark at the same person the fiftieth time that he comes to the door as loudly as he did the first time. The least confinement is the best with the typical vocal small dog. An inside bedding container or mat is usually adequate. If these dogs live only with adults they generally don't need a crate. However, they often have low tolerance for children or roughhousing and in this instance may require a place of seclusion, such as a crate, to be able to get away for a peaceful nap.

What about the yard dog? We see little value for this flea collector which usually develops an obsession for chasing cars, running a fence, barking incessantly or sneaking a bite from a child that inappropriately gets near his fence. This is not a dog well utilized in an urban setting. Unless you expect a burglar to steal your lawn furniture or vandalize your landscaping, he has little value. His haphazard barking will not alert you to a real threat. He has already barked equally loud at the neighbor's dog, garbage man, bird, and passing autos. Unless your house is totally surrounded by a yard, it is evident to the most inept felon that he only need enter your home from a window or door outside the fence of the dog's yard.

The country cousin of the yard dog, the outside farm dog, generally is of greater use. The farm dog serves to drive off predators endangering poultry or livestock, and is the early warning device for the occupants of the home. This rural canine cousin, like the other livestock, has his place and purpose and it is not in the house!

Dr. Edward Weiss. Dr. Weiss is a graduate of Chicago Medical School and has been involved in cardiovascular research at Washington University in St. Louis. At present he is in the private practice of Cardiology in St. Louis, where he lives with his wife, Barbara, and their three sons.

Manners

Manners are usually only recognized in a dog when they are bad. A dog with bad manners is an irritation to everyone. Your puppy (like an infant or small child) requires constant and complete supervision. If you are not in a position to watch or supervise him put him away. A puppy's conduct should not intrude on your life. If your puppy causes you to put down your book, excuse yourself during a telephone conversation, or interrupt your dinner his manners need to be improved. He should not be destructive in your home, annoy friends or cause discomfort and confusion by his uncontrolled exuberance and enthusiastic affection. We do not accept muddy foot prints and saliva drenched clothing no matter how happy the dog is when we come through the door. A well mannered dog provides companionship without disturbing your environment. This tranquility is an important aspect of a gratifying relationship between a man and his dog.

To protect this tranquility there must be established rules of canine etiquette. The following big ten doggy **'don'ts'** are problems we have encountered which either singly or in combination, have wrecked many a happy pet home.

Imagine what a combination of these bad manners can do. Canines who have acquired one or several of the Big Ten cause church-going people to swear, blood pressures to rise, and loving owners to abuse their "best friends." Dog lovers swear they will never get another dog. The lady of the house utters those famous words "either the dog goes or I do!"

To a great extent these problems are avoidable. The cliche, "an ounce of prevention is worth a pound of cure," cannot be more graphically demonstrated than with the Big Ten bad habits of some companion dogs. We hope to provide you with a method for prevention and, if necessary, the more difficult procedures for effecting their cure.

Your dog may attempt to outwit you by doing in your absence what he would not do in your presence and you must employ certain useful tricks. We have set mouse traps next to objects we do not want the dog to touch. Results have been gratifying.

It is much more difficult to correct bad habits than to train correctly from the beginning. Bad habits are formed when you consciously or unconsciously allow your dog to do something destructive without correction. A bad habit is born and receives your seal of approval unless you actively stop him in the act.

Our goal is to avoid the formation of bad habits, rather than correcting them once they have been established. An unsupervised young dog will quickly develop an impressive repertoire of bad habits. Playtime must be supervised! When you are otherwise engaged and cannot supervise, the young dog should be kept in his crate, dog run/kennel, or similar type of regulated enclosure.

1) Tearing up your home, yard, pool toys etc., and giving you the pain of shredded curtains, chewed furniture, destroyed clothing etc.

This problem develops because the dog is entertaining himself. It is "fun" for your dog to play in the house. The dog must be taught what he can and cannot do in your home. Your constant supervision is required to direct and discipline your puppy to understand the activities that are forbidden and those that are allowed. A dog learns by trial and error. Pain versus pleasure is his motivation. The joys of chewing a leather shoe seem marvelous to the puppy. One shoe is the same as another to your dog, therefore your new shoes will suit him just as well as the discarded slipper you gave him to play with.

To train your dog not to chew, we recommend providing a substitute. This substitute may be a rawhide bone, or hard rubber toy. All else is forbidden! This black and white approach makes it much easier for the dog to decide in your absence what he may do. Since there are so many objects that can provide fun for your dog, it will require months of attentive observation and training to have a trustworthy pet.

2) Stains, stench, and the hidden surprise of no toilet responsibility.

We feel the most important "tool" essential for house breaking is the dog crate. The dog crate takes advantage of the dog's natural instinct, not to foul the place he sleeps. We have housebroken dogs in a matter of days with the use of a crate. When you let the dog out of the crate, yet not out of the house, he will prepare to make a mistake in the house. An immediate correction must be made, and then take the dog outside without delay. The dog must learn to communicate to you that he wants to go out of the house. Consistency is of the utmost importance! Allowing a mistake can undo many days, or weeks, of correct training. In the early stages of housebreaking the puppy you will be making numerous corrections. The closer your consistency is to one hundred percent immediate corrections, the quicker the puppy will get the message.. If you are a poor supervisor your puppy will be confused, learn slowly, and have to endure numerous corrections.

3) The yammering, howling, or midnight serenade—canine sound pollution.

The dog engages in this unacceptable behavior because it's fun and (most likely) gets your attention. If noise-making continues without prompt human intervention then the dog is serenading the neighborhood. If he stops with human intervention then his noise-making is for human attention. Noise-making is most easily stopped in its early stages regardless of the reason. We stop him with a stern voice command, "NO!" accompanied by a physical correction (collar jerk), planning later to use only a vocal correction.

The most caring people, often by mistake, teach this noisy habit to their dog on his first night at home. The young puppy's first night in their home is one of whining and screaming, as he seeks attention and reassurance in a strange place. If you respond to the dog's cry for help you are training him to call for you whenever he wishes. You must make the hard choice of ignoring the poor puppy. This may seem heartless, but if not done you are on the way to becoming your dog's servant. One should learn the difference between the dogs barking to be allowed out to relieve himself versus the bark for attention. This difference is often obvious as the uncomfortable animal is active and restless in the crate. The lonesome dog is often lying motionless and whining in a rhythmic way.

If your dog is barking while he is in the back yard or pen then it is best to keep him tied. It is much easier to catch him when he is tied. When the barking starts pass through the back door yelling, "Quiet, quiet," over and over as you run to the dog. As you catch him, still yelling "Quiet," grasp the tie close to his collar and jerk back and forth to make an uncomfortable correction. If this does not work then your correction is not strong enough.

4) Disobedience - ignoring your command to come, sit, going deaf when he hears your voice.

Dogs are MASTERS of the deaf ear! This canine actor is so convincing that we have seen their owners become hoarse from shouting at their dogs in obedience class. Folks have even come to dog obedience classes asking for special attention because the poor thing is deaf! Don't be fooled. It is rare for a dog not to have the most acute hearing, until he is extremely old. The hard of hearing dog just requires an incentive to listen, rather than a hearing aid. When he responds to your voice, he is paying attention to you.

Your dog MUST pay attention to you before you can train him. You have to be tough! Dogs are just like us, unless you show them a reason, either bribe or correction, they will not interrupt what they are doing to respond to your requests. The "deaf" dog will develop incredibly acute hearing in a good obedience class.

5) Running away from home. This includes sneaking out through a cracked door, jumping fences, and generally pretending he knows no real boundaries.

Exploration and looking for rivals, or dates, is part of being a dog! This is against our rules. Many people restrain their dogs to prevent this activity. Since no restraint is one hundred percent effective they often find themselves placing ads for lost dogs. They are avoiding the problem, not correcting it.

This problem will be solved when your dog responds dependably when called. Learning the "recall," which means coming to you on command, is the most fundamental obedience exercise. It must be practiced until the dog responds automatically and without hesitation. In a good dog obedience class planned distractions are used to lure dogs into making mistakes while the trainer has control. Distraction is difficult to control when training alone at home or in any uncontrolled environment. A dog is considered to be trained or under control when he responds to your commands despite distractions. A trained dog is a pleasure to be with. You can be confident that he will come when called, and this allows the dog much greater freedom and you will have a 'companion' rather than a 'captive.'

Fence-jumping can be prevented by having either a twelve foot fence secured in concrete or a trained dog. It is possible to prevent fence-jumping through supervision and subsequent training rather than restraint. The dog that encounters a painful correction on the **first** attempt to climb or jump over the fence will not do it again. You can accomplish this by using a long line (fifteen feet or more) attached to your dog's collar and jerking smartly as the dog jumps. For greatest effect you should either be out of sight or make the dog think you aren't paying any attention. In the past the long line was our only tool to correct a dog at a distance away from us. Its limitations are obvious. We must hold the line which prevents us from hiding while waiting for the dog to make his move.

The electronic training collar is now available and is the ultimate long distance correction. This small battery-powered unit will permit you to correct your dog at distances up to several hundred yards. Clearly it is unsurpassed in preventing problems such as fence jumping. You may stay within your home out of sight of the dog and correct him while he is outside by pressing a button! This is a two-part device in which the trainer holds a small radio transmitter and the dog wears an electronic receiver on his collar. The drawbacks are the initial expense of its purchase and the effort required to learn its proper use.

Proper usage means understanding that it is important that the dog does not know where the correction comes from. For this reason he can think it was an insect bite or simply something painful but without associating it with you. In this case he will seek to avoid that area or whatever he thinks may have caused the pain. The dog's desire to flee can confuse your training. For example a dog that is electronically corrected when not responding to a recall command, may run away from rather than to his trainer. We emphasize this, as we have found this electronic aid to be most helpful in reinforcing rather than introducing new commands.

6) Stealing. This is the all too frequent doggie attempt to snatch food from the table or take away any object that smells interesting, such as your leather wallet, shoes, or purse. Sometimes we only find out about it, when several days later his hidden booty is found.

To stop "stealing" we must teach the dog "crime does not pay!" This means that we must catch the dog in the act and correct him immediately. If the dog is sensitive, often only one or two such corrections may be needed.

The problem is a smart dog steals only when we are not there and thus avoids correction. Like a burglar these dogs get what they want by stealth.

Two approaches are effective in stopping this canine thief. The first is based on good obedience training. This is a long, preventative process taking months of conscientious supervision. A dog trained this way has learned to pay attention to what YOU want and understand the rules of the house.

Another method which works to help explain the rules of the house is to incorporate the use of a mouse trap. In this method of attitude adjustment a tempting morsel is placed on a paper plate carefully positioned on top of a mouse trap. When the dog disturbs the plate he is rudely shocked by the sudden noise, or worse.

TABLE MANNERS

LONESOME

7) The canine "brat." This dog tries to get his way by frightening you.

The same displays of aggression we would hope would be used to protect us are turned against us by the brat. Frequently this is begun in adolescence and becomes more extreme each time the dog succeeds. This dog can become extremely dangerous to his owner. He is confident in his ability to intimidate members of the household to get his way. We have had to rescue owners from this type of canine tyrant. These dogs are not inhibited from inflicting pain or fear to their owners. They dominate the household, taking advantage of sensitive, softhearted owners. This is the classic "spare the rod spoil the dog" example.

The problem begins in what appears to be a cute feisty puppy. It is easy to overlook and excuse the dog that guards his bone, is reluctant to give up his spot on the couch, or barks at the dinner table for a treat. For some people it is easier to give in to these situations than to resist. Permitting yourself to be pushed around by your dog is WRONG and will result in your harboring a 'brat.' If he is not stopped decisively this dog will push harder and unbelievable results can occur. We have seen a dog that eventually claimed the second floor of his home, where the people usually slept! Another canine brat was able to train his owner to feed him with alternate fork-fulls of food from the owners plate during mealtime. Neither of these situations happened overnight. The dogs slowly demanded and got more each week. If denied they became progressively more aggressive and threatening until they gained what they wanted.

Aggression must be nipped in the bud! Your dog has no right to growl, snarl, or snap at you. Correct him, and teach him which one of you runs the household. We can only emphasize it is much easier to do this with a small puppy than it is with a ninety-five pound, muscular, confident canine bruiser.

8) A dog and/or cat 'Bully.' You do not want your dog to become the canine terror of the neighborhood, bringing home parts of your neighbor's pets. Just like the dog described above this one acts aggressively but targets animals. Your neighbor's pets are likely to be his victims.

This problem often takes place when the owner regards his dog's right to roam as normal behavior. It is particularly bad when the same owner thinks that his canine bully is only giving proof of his value as a protection dog. Nothing could be further from the truth. Dog-aggressive animals usually are not protective of humans. They roam and fight for their own selfish purposes and do not bother themselves with things like intruders that might bother you.

Canine aggression becomes more pronounced the more freedom a dog has and the more he can act without supervision. Dogs that roam, learn to think for themselves and handle themselves independently—especially around other dogs. Their pack instincts become sharpened. A dog that is his own boss all day long, may not care to hear your opinion at night.

The dominant dog when left to roam may lead a pack of dogs into serious trouble. We know of a German Shepherd that led a pack of dogs in killing animals in a metropolitan zoo and successfully eluded police and park rangers for several months. Small herd animals such as Gazelles were cornered in their compounds and maimed by the pack.

This behavior has been reported to lead to attacks on human beings. Children can become prey to these animals with horrible consequences. Lack of training and neglect are always found as characteristics shared by the owners of these dogs.

Prevention of this problem behavior is accomplished by not permitting dogs to roam free, and supervising their interaction with other dogs. Dogs that demonstrate aggression to other dogs are the ones most in need of obedience training classes. Here they are taught to pay attention to their owners, while being tempted by the other dogs in the class. In class the dog learns very quickly that he does not have the freedom to do as he pleases. If he lunges or acts aggressively toward the other dogs, he will receive severe corrections from his owner. Human orientation rather than canine orientation is made the goal of training. When the dog appears not to be paying attention, he is usually seeking to visit, sniff, and interact with the other dogs. This behavior is also corrected and paying attention to you becomes his most important duty. His attention will be riveted on his owner even though he may be in close proximity with two other dogs.

9) Hysteria, hyperactivity.

Hyperactivity in dogs is a nuisance. It can be seen in the household that allows its dog to run wildly because he has so much energy. These people are "teaching" their dog that running in circles, bouncing off

100

the couch, leaping at the walls and people is an acceptable aerobic outlet. No dog has too much energy, he is only manifesting uncontrolled behavior. The same animal that appears high strung and unable to sit still would gladly trade this behavior for a chance at retrieving a ball or a similar activity.

In obedience class we eliminate this behavior by teaching a dog to lie in one position until it is excused. Frequently we reward this show of self control with play.

10) The Friendly Canine Clod.

This big "galoot" jumps up and licks you in the face and as you wipe off the saliva you are reassured, "I think he likes you!" This pest is the product of an indulgent owner and undisciplined home environment. He is frequently looked upon by his owners as a "furry child." Since he means no harm why should he be corrected and have his feelings hurt. These people often confuse correcting a dog with destroying his friendliness. They must learn that their dog will not reject them and sulk if he is not allowed to slobber over them and others. Many techniques have been employed to push the dog down or even to grab his paws and hold him standing in order to stop his bad habit. We have found that simply teaching and enforcing the sit command is the most effective method to correct this behavior. The dog soon learns the best way to avoid obedience commands is to be a little more reserved.

For this German Shepherd, the Station Wagon is HIS territory. Intruders beware!

Thomas G. Rose at his training kennel in St. Louis. Thomas G. Rose and his wife, Holly, live in St. Louis. They own the Dog House Kennel Inc. where they maintain an active breeding program for their German Shepherds.

Both Tom and Holly are presently engaged in teaching competitive dog training and conducting Schutzhund seminars. In addition the Roses conduct a trade school course for professional dog trainers at The Dog House. Tom also serves as Training Director of the Spirit of St. Louis Schutzhund Club. This club's winning record with personally raised and trained dogs is unequaled in America.

Finding Your Puppy—"Doing It Yourself"

The best way to have "the perfect protective dog" is to do it yourself under the supervision of a professional trainer, who is "in tune" with your goals. In this way you will change the puppy into the dog who will share your life and protect you. The skilled professional trainer who works with you will help you develop this relationship between you and your dog. "Doing it yourself" means doing it properly with guidance. Mastery of this training skill requires experience and personal (one-on-one) instruction.

Many people are not willing to invest the time to acquire skill in dog training. This does not mean these people cannot have a good dog. It does mean that they should never seek to own a dog that will bite or demonstrate a level of aggression they are unqualified to manage. One important warning: DO NOT PURCHASE A KNOWN BITING DOG UNLESS YOU KNOW FROM EXPERIENCE HOW TO HANDLE HIM, or ARE PREPARED TO INVEST A GREAT DEAL OF TIME WITH A PROFESSIONAL TRAINER LEARNING HOW TO HANDLE AND MAINTAIN HIM. If you want the **"real thing,"** you must master the skills to develop him and have the competence to maintain him. Neither this skill nor competence can be bought. It must be earned through dedication and effort. The type of mastery needed to own the "real thing" requires developing your personal skill in dog training—a type of training that is **mandatory** for anyone who would own "the real thing," and highly advisable to anyone who truly wants to develop his skill beyond a superficial level.

One on one (private) instruction is rarely discussed when the subject of dog training is presented. Very few books on the subject attempt to distinguish dog training classes from private lessons. The difference is immense! In almost any field requiring the development of skill, a coach (trainer) will move his pupil more rapidly and efficiently than the same trainer can accomplish with a group.

It is surprising that direct instruction for the future dog owner and trainer is so rare when this type of training has become so popular in many other sports. One of our children spent six months in a tennis clinic noted for good instruction and yet showed rather mediocre improvement. In contrast, this child, after a single private lesson with a tennis pro, dramatically enhanced his game. The pro corrected bad habits and created drills that could be performed in solitary practice in order to sharpen the child's skills. This kind of personal training is rarely sought out because of the preconceptions of how expensive it must be. Economics dictate that group classes are less expensive than private instruction, but one willing to assume the expense of maintaining a dog for a decade or more may find this difference smaller than imagined.

Some people are simply unaware that private instruction is available. Anyone who truly wishes to have a protection dog that will protect beyond barking will ultimately require private lessons. The reasons for this include the fact that training dogs in protection work is a noisy business. The dogs bark and the dog owner may find that shouting is the only way to be heard by the instructor. Additionally there is a safety principle that requires the instructor to give his undivided attention to a dog behaving aggressively.

The class situation for protection training is more of a supplemental rather than a beginning method for training. As the owner becomes more sophisticated and can assume responsibility for the dog's behavior then the presence of other people during training becomes less hazardous.

For some people who begin training their dogs as protection animals, the development of their own training skill becomes a reward in itself. These people will often seek another avenue for demonstrating and testing their ability in dog training. They enter competitions which evaluate their training skill and their dog's ability. Dog shows, obedience trials, field trials, and the Scutzhund Sport are the present arenas of canine competition in the world. It is from these events that the conformation, character, and training techniques for future generations of dogs will be codified. Dog trainers now have available opportunities unknown to breeders and trainers of only thirty years ago. Technology, including video tapes, radio controlled equipment, ever improved communication between dog fanciers, and incorporation of the advances in behavioral psychology and genetics, all allow us to continue to develop ever better dogs.

As the child is father to the man, so is the puppy father to the dog. The importance of puppy development for creation of the truly exceptional canine companion has been recognized by those who train competitive dogs. Puppy development is not passive, but an opportunity to begin shaping the future adult canine companion. It has long been recognized in children that early environmental influence has a profound effect on the adult person. It is for these reasons that so much attention is now being directed toward pre-school education. We can borrow from what has been learned in the area of early human education and apply it to our puppies in training. This has already been done by some of our most successful dog trainers.

Complex obedience routines are seen demonstrated in the sport of Schutzhund, KNPV, and ringsport—to mention a few. In these sports the dog is required to perform difficult protection routines yet always under complete control of the handler.

One does not have to be a Protection Dog sports participant to understand how these seemingly conflicting behaviors can be possessed by the same dog. The ability to display both combativeness and sophisticated obedience was nurtured at a very young age. This flies in the face of the "let the dog be a dog" school of dog training. The natural instincts of the puppy are channeled into behavior the trainer deems suitable. The puppy's desire to bite is encouraged but directed to inanimate objects such as a burlap sack or toy. This early work also includes teaching the puppy to let go on command (control). The training pays off in later years by producing a dog that will appear to ferociously seize and hold a padded sleeve and—in the midst of what appears a raging fight—will, upon command, instantly release the hold and sit.

There are certain important observations that must be made. It is necessary for dog owners to cultivate their puppy into a dog which will obey them without hesitation, yet retain his protective character. It is a mistaken idea that obedience training creates submission and fear. Quite the opposite is true.

Dog sport's competition immediately thrusts upon the dog trainer the challenge of raising an animal which can simultaneously maintain the character, courage and stability required for man-work, plus the attentiveness and discipline needed for successful obedience, and the drive/desire to succeed that the truly excellent tracking dog maintains. To accomplish all of this in a single dog requires a mixture of "inductive" and "compulsive" training so as to allow confidence to develop in the dog and his self-control to mature. Aspects of this puppy training can therefore be used by anyone seeking to attain these attributes in creating the desired companion/protector dog.

The most important decision facing the new puppy owner is how to raise and train him to produce the perfect mature companion. A dog so trained will be confident and love to please his owner. This will serve us whether we want the perfect dog for our home that will LOVE AND PROTECT or one who will go on to participate in the world of dog sports competition. Not everyone can drive and enjoy to its fullest potential a race-tuned Ferrari, but one does not need to limit oneself to the canine equivalent of an automatic four-cylinder economy car for his leisure and pleasure. The dog that "could" be trained for National competition is a joy to own.

The careful selection of blood lines and strict attention to training technique will be vital only to competitive dog trainers. However, the opportunity to purchase the same bloodlines and utilize proven resources within the animal is an asset available to anyone willing to spend time in the selection process. The training principals employed by the "Pros" can be used by ANYONE willing to learn them. Basic techniques for developing boxing skills may be learned as the fundamentals of self defense—one need not become a professional prize fighter in order to benefit from them. Not everyone intends to spend the time and effort necessary to train a competitive working dog, but using proven techniques to develop a dog who will be something more than a fireside ornament can be of benefit to you and your canine family member. Even more important is the fact that if the early training is bypassed certain valuable aspects of the dog's character development will be lost forever.

Breeding

How can we find THE puppy which is the best "raw material." It all begins with breeding. Geneticists tell us that human temperament is an almost indivisible mixture of **nature** and **nurture.** As dog trainers, it is fortunate for us that this mixture is more easily divisible in our canine pupils. We can short-circuit many eons of evolution by selective breeding. This power is an obvious two-edged sword. We can intensify and concentrate both mental and physical characteristics to suit our needs. It is unfortunate that this power greatly exceeds our wisdom. It requires an expert trainer to know the characteristics that should be sought. Breeders can often be misled by fad, fancy or pure "kennel-blindness" (a wide-spread disease).

In order to select the best characteristics in our breeding we must first understand **dog training**! For the individual who has never trained a dog it is difficult to evaluate and recognize the characteristics necessary in a puppy that later will produce the ideal mature dog. This "best" choice will differ only in minor respects between individual trainers. One trainer may want higher energy, higher drive, while another trainer stresses different criteria. The basic interest remains the same, and that is the innate trainability of the dog that will translate into working ability. We feel that the inherited basis of this working ability must be identified by the breeder in his own stock in order for him to reproduce it in a consistent way. It may also be identified by the non-breeder who has worked with enough examples of both good and poor working ability. This working ability is the basis for correct breeding. One can imagine the difficulty of trying to select a pup for working ability if one has never trained a dog (or very many dogs). This is as difficult as trying to select fast horses if one has never been involved with horse racing or even seen a horse race. Many breeders who are quite well known in the show ring readily admit they are not interested in dog training. They restrict themselves to producing beautiful animals. Thus seeking a working or potentially protective dog from them is comparable to trying to get a race horse from someone who breeds beautiful walking horses.

A sad but necessary comment is that dog breeders of the working/ herding dogs in this country are divided into "show breeders" or "working breeders." Frequently these breeders are financially well off and do a lot of advertising. Unfortunately some "show" breeders sell structurally inferior, genetically flawed, and even psychotic dogs as their "working stock" in contrast to their "show dogs." They usually breed specifically for winning conformation structure—the rejects are dubbed "working dogs." Advertisements of these breeders can be identified because they announce "working and show puppies" out of championship bloodlines. They are willing to discount the price of the "pet" or "working prospects!" (As you will have seen in this book, characteristics of genetic temperament can be tested by an expert and categorized at a very young age. Only through testing can the suitability of a specific puppy be determined.)

Another group selling dogs is the well-intentioned naive breeder who rarely trains, and is emotionally prejudiced against dog training. They produce at the ring of a bell (their own telephone) a working prospect. The combination of these breeder types has done far more harm to our "working breeds" than the regularly maligned backyard breeder and the "puppy mill." Unfortunately ignorance and greed are associated with most human activities, including dog breeding.

Probably the most irresponsible person from whom to buy a dog is the self-appointed working dog expert who never trains, never competes, but is a gifted, articulate salesperson. This person is out to make money, and does.

Puppies—Training and Socialization

There is something attractive about beginning with a well-chosen puppy. Hopefully with the above information, you will have avoided the inferior puppy sold to you as a discounted "working type" from either an ignorant or dishonest breeder. You will have obtained a puppy whose parents are of sound health and who may have had working titles either in Schutzhund or obedience sports, or who at the very least, is closely related to such dogs.

The future "real thing" puppy will be a blank page when he comes to your home. You will be able to shape this puppy to your needs more completely and achieve more with him than you could with any adult dog. This "simpatico" will include the puppy's knowing and loving his "littermates," which are your children, loving the hand that feeds him (usually the lady of the house), and becoming the alpha wolf in your absence, guarding all that you hold precious. This process takes as much thought and care as does raising a child to become a productive member of society. This puppy must grow into a confident adult and yet NOT BE ALLOWED to dominate his human family. You cannot hope to be away from the dog for long periods of time (weeks or months) during the critical period of eight weeks to one year and still accomplish what you want. If you are starting with a puppy we strongly recommend that you seek professional guidance from a "well qualified" local trainer. This can't be Aunt Tilly of miniature Poodle fame, the guy down the block who takes his dog hunting once a year, or the policeman who works in the Canine Corps. You need a person who trains dogs for a living—one who can present you with a list of accomplishments to authenticate his expertise. Hopefully, dog training will be his passion as well as his profession. You will be doubly rewarded if he is the one that bred and sold you the puppy.

You should understand that many preconceived ideas of dog training will be shattered during this early experience with your trainer.

Raising the puppy to any protective level yet keeping him as a family dog will require daily input, weekly formal training, and will ultimately produce the type of animal that you could not purchase as an adult. This animal can be thought of as "customized" for you. Just as the most expensive clothes and personal items are those that are one of a kind and made just for one customer, so has this dog been "made" **only** for you in your home. What customized him was your effort in selection, and the ongoing training and shaping of his temperament to meet your needs. A protective dog purchased as "ready made" can never take your dog's place. The only advantage of the "ready made" is that he can be purchased quickly and conveniently—for those who do not want to (or cannot) invest the time and effort that is essential when you train your own pup.

The basis of this book, however, is that it is not wise for anyone seeking a protective dog for their family pet to own a commercial guard dog. For this reason puppy training and temperament evaluation is presented for those who will be "do-it-yourselfers."

Just as one would not attempt to learn how to safely scuba dive only from reading a manual, one cannot and should not train a protective, biting dog solely from using a book. In later chapters we will describe the methods of training that will guide owners to producing a dog suitable for their needs. We believe it unnecessary and dangerous to give "how to" lessons in attack training. People who are seeking this type of training will require "hands on" help from a well-qualified professional dog trainer. His qualifications and training skills can better be judged by those who have mastered the dynamics of canine temperament and motivation described in later chapters.

Training—Socialization

The development of a protection dog requires genetic potential and the molding of that genetic background to interact with its environment in a predictable and controlled manner. This molding is the essence of training. Capturing the fundamental drives of the dog and channeling them into a behavior that we seek is the most efficient, lasting and effective manner of dog training. The first drive we must recognize is the dog's desire to play. His play can consist of exploration, retrieval, mock battle, and that most difficult to describe action, his desire to please. When deciding to train a dog, the age at which this training begins dictates the most effective mode of training to employ. With the young puppy, training is so non-structured that it is often

LEARNING EXPERIENCE

described as socialization. It may be argued that socialization (allowing a puppy to see different people, things, and places), is not training. But one only needs to see a dog that has been constantly confined to a kennel to understand how fundamental is the dog's 'socialization.' Socialization of the puppy is what puts the sparkle in his eye. It is the foundation for everything that is to come.

Socialization is accomplished by positive exposure. The puppy sees different people, walks over different surfaces, is fondled, carried—and never hurt. Seeing, hearing, and having his actions positively reinforced creates the confidence in himself he needs to deal with the stresses he will find in his later life. The most important **myth** to destroy is that isolation of the dog at a young age will increase his ability and inclination to be protective. Inexperienced dog handlers often refuse to let anyone else touch their puppy in a misguided effort to make their dog "protective." This ploy only creates a maladjustment in a normally social pack animal. This animal will not behave as a working companion of man, but will revert more to behavior associated with wild beasts. This dog will not seek you as company, he will shrink from touch, not seek to confront a stranger but will withdraw. His aggression will only occur as it does in the wild state when all exits are blocked. There is one possible use for this animal if one happens to inherit one. If confined to a territory he will sound an alert as his anxiety is raised by the approaching stranger. He will, however, be no more protective of your property or of you than any other wild animal. Similarly, canines taken in from the wild—wolves and wolf mixes—are not protective except of themselves. The non-socialized dog is not confident when confronted with strange sounds, does not seek to confront strangers, and will withdraw or hide if given the opportunity. No, a wolf or wolf mix is not better than a properly socialized dog for protection or companionship.

Socialization accomplishes a redirection of the pack drive to the human being as a pack member. It reinforces the working relationship between man and dog. A contract of mutual adoration is developed at this age. It is best in early training that human contact be emphasized and contact with other canines restricted or eliminated. In short, do not raise the puppy with another puppy or adult dog. Your bond with the puppy is not strengthened by his having to compete with another puppy or adult dog for your attention in his home. The other dog is going to win this competition! More than one dog in a household does not improve trainability. Socialization is best accomplished without the distraction of another animal providing examples in behavior that you do not seek to reproduce. An older dog does not show the younger one the way—except in "doggy" things. Retrieving a dumbbell on command, walking on lead, and learning to turn loose of what they are holding are not "doggy" things. Possibly biting is reinforced by imitation but letting go on command is not.

A. Play Training

The most fundamental task for the future protective dog owner is how this animal will be forged from a squirming puppy. The dog will require the correct mixture of positive attitude coupled with respect for the trainer. The positive attitude is initiated with play training. It is not the attitude of "let him be a puppy, grow up, and enjoy life—plenty of time for training later." It is the beginning of play-training which shapes the training relationship. Play-training is positive, it can involve food, toys, objects of curiosity, and roughhousing.

Food should not be readily available to the puppy so that he is always stuffed. We recommend that at feeding time the food be made available for four minutes and then be withdrawn until the next scheduled feeding. Food treats must be linked to behavior that you encourage such as coming when called.

Ball chasing is a wonderful occupation for the young puppy. Just as with food, the ball should not be always available, but should always

Very little coaxing needed with good retriever.

be associated with your presence. The ball in your hand, quickly thrown, creates a camaraderie and your appearance is a joyful anticipation of play. You are now setting the stage for further steps of this training-socialization period.

A natural extension of play-training for the future protection animal is rough-housing or tussling. Tussling means roughing up his fur, patting him, turning him over, but NOT holding him down against his will or dominating him. Your puppy should be subordinate to you but not SUBMISSIVE to you. It is our observation that as long as he is "coming back for more" the puppy is having a positive interplay with his owner. The end of this game should be petting the puppy, scratching his stomach or simply standing up and walking away. Many puppies will, during tussling, bite, grab at sleeves and cuffs, and their needle-teeth will remind you when they need to be directed to a towel, rag, or puppy pull-toy as they continue to act out their biting. If it is difficult to redirect the puppy from your skin to a toy, then you can permit or even encourage the puppy to bite your hand, and while he is biting push his lips against his sharp teeth causing discomfort—a negative reinforcement. This correction should not be accompanied by a verbal scolding because we want the puppy to believe that the act of biting caused the pain, not you!

The concept of allowing the puppy to bite goes against the grain of common knowledge. Common knowledge, however, does not train dogs. In reality, early extinguishing of a puppy's biting will make a potentially suitable companion, but his protective ability in the house will be equal to that of any indoor piece of furniture. So we recognize we are not going to slap the puppy that bites, NOR correct him vigorously but rather seek to redirect his biting to an inanimate object such as a towel, rag, toy, etc. The ability to accomplish this is no small task. We all reflexively strike out when nipped and it is **our** reaction that needs to be retrained. We are aware that this concept flies in the face of people who train "good dogs." Good dogs, however, are in the eyes of the beholder, and as we will discuss later, this biting is still an extension of instinctual prey training which is then easily directed in the older dog to biting a sleeve.

The "sleeve" is a heavily padded tube worn over the forearm which is used in training dogs to bite on command or in response to an aggressor. The sleeve-biting is a building block in the development of the "real thing," but need not be carried out beyond the point of a game

113

playing ritual. This game playing can become so stylized that a dog will bite only a sleeve, and would not consider biting a person not so equipped.

B. Prey Training

The dog is a carnivore and deep within his genes—be he Pekinese or Pointer—he has the desire to hunt. Prey training is not the use of live objects, but rather an imitation of the 'stalk and chase' in a directed manner.

Prey-training is a natural extension of play-training. A dog's normal predatory instinct is to chase. It is the way his ancestors earned their living! This very basic drive is easily revived in even the youngest puppy by having him chase an article of interest to him which is attached to a string and drawn across the floor. You will see him stalk, charge, grab, and cavort in an ecstasy of hunting delight. Prey training is a very important ingredient of protection training. No, he is not fed gunpowder, beaten by strangers, kept isolated in the dark, chained to a tree, or made to smell blood. Instead he is allowed to chase somebody in a game-like fashion who retreats when the puppy or young dog advances. This retreat causes the prey instinct to surface and only when a young dog is straining at the leash and trying to reach a retreating stranger will he ever be allowed to get close enough to grab the rag or burlap sack the stranger is fluttering before him. It is the same fluttering sack and inanimate object that began in his play- training and was carried out in prey-training that becomes the impetus for his predatory dominance in these mock theatrics.

C. Defensive Training—"The Real Thing"

Most impressions of guard dog training evoke images of a dog being threatened. Threatening the dog is a method of defensive training. Defensive training is the "Bogeyman" of creating a protective dog. Unlike our other types of training it evokes a **NEGATIVE** feeling in the dog and then converts the feeling of fear or self defense to make the dog ferocious. In defensive training, the dog is not chasing prey or playing with an object, but acting out a fear. In defensive training anxiety is produced in the dog by threat. It is an incredibly delicate stimulus which is so modulated as to cause the dog to be fearful, yet not so fearful that the dog retreats. As can be readily deduced this modulation requires an **EXPERT** trainer who is able to accurately read the response of a particular dog much as a psychologist can understand approach-avoidance feelings in human beings.

114

"Prey Training." Puppy chases and bites to catch rather than defend.

This is the first time that fear has been introduced as a training stimulus. This training should only be undertaken by those who insist on "the real thing." It will create a dog that bites people. We do not intend to give a "Malicious Mauler-101" general survey course on this subject. It is important, however, to realize the two components needed to successfully carry it off. These components are: 1) An expert trainer. 2) A dog that has been developed since puppyhood with this intent.

We do believe it is valuable to distinguish DEFENSIVE TRAINING from other forms of training. Defensive training is a type of training that will not be successful unless the dog has the genetic potential to be able to withstand stress. This genetic potential must have been previously molded, utilizing the confidence development inherent in socialization, play-training, and prey-training as building blocks for this final step.

It is indeed a last step that need not be carried out in order to have a sound alert dog or a dog that will stand protectively in his territory and hold an intruder at bay by barking at him.

PUPPY TESTING

116

Puppy Training—
Temperament and Character Development

Until now this book has been devoted to the matter of choosing the best puppy for you. Once the choice is made and you have your puppy at home his development and training will depend on you.

Instilling a positive attitude in the dog is very important. It is with this goal in mind that we begin the program of character development by the use of games and positive training.

The training games described in this chapter are ones with which we have had success in building confidence, energy, outgoing attitude, and enthusiasm in our young dogs. Early training focuses on building confidence without allowing the puppy to be the boss. This can be accomplished with a blend of obedience training and games designed to increase the dog's self determination.

Most of these games are designed for a dog that is an ACTIVE MEMBER of your home. These techniques are useful to produce a companion who will obey, enjoy playing games, and will mature with a serious attitude about protection. They are not needed to produce an adequate sound alert dog nor are they a requirement in developing an intimidating but harmless gentle giant.

Some trainers believe that the best way to raise the puppy is with the LEAST amount of control. "Let him be a puppy and grow up and enjoy life—plenty of time for training later," seems to be a common opinion. Socializing in this context often refers to a broad spectrum of events and activities, with few being planned, that take place in the puppy's development. To these trainers, socializing merely involves keeping the puppy with you so he can be exposed to many different situations. Frequently no guidance is given in teaching the puppy how to react to various situations.

A desirable protective companion dog is NOT an accident. Rather, he is the result of a consistent, flexible training program that starts at the earliest possible age, with a puppy of proven genetic potential. The training program is adapted to the puppy's own developing characteristics. You have a chosen a puppy who you hope will follow in his parent's footsteps. The parents are not simply abstract names on a pedigree. Their "get" will be the raw material with which we will seek to build and mold in order to obtain the dog you want.

Raising and training the puppy will be an interaction between dog and human designed to produce the ideal dog. The effective trainer will minimize the accidental factors and supplant them with well-planned, thought-out experiences. These experiences will familiarize the young dog with the future skills he will eventually acquire which are necessary for him to be able to perform when he assumes his role as protector of your home. We call this strategic training plan "socializing."

Different places and situations must be used to socialize a dog and make him at ease wherever he may be called upon. You should avoid developing a dog who acts appropriately only in a narrow environment (such as the training center) and is confused and unpredictable when he accompanies you in public. This confidence and trainability conditioning is used as a process of environmental adaptation. The socializing process avoids producing a dog that cowers, lunges, or barks inappropriately. The more experiences the young puppy has the better!

You want to arrange for the puppy to be victorious in all new situations—he always wins. Thus, each new situation represents a positive learning experience for him. To accomplish this the trainer MUST be able to "read" the puppy—and reading the puppy is no easy task. The effective trainer will develop the ability to recognize the point at which the puppy is "going over the edge,"—becoming fearful of the new situation. This edge or threshold is frequently encountered in each new situation, but the constructive trainer will recover at the last minute and turn it into a positive experience. The happy dog as a personal protection dog or as a police dog is, first of all, a confident dog.

Training techniques are not intended to create a marionette with a dejected or anxious appearance. The protector and companion dog must be raised to be a happy, confident animal. To accomplish this submission, fear, and isolation must be carefully and deliberately avoided.

People sometimes confuse an animal's submission with learning to obey. They are not the same. Trainablity is cultivated by preserving the dog's enthusiasm and diminished by teaching him to avoid the training situation.

We have witnessed, after the first training session, an incredible difference in how dogs return to training. Some dogs, within a week of "homework" with their owners, balk, scream, and struggle to escape the horrors of training. While other dogs bound happily from their cars as they return to the training facility. Obviously something very different has been experienced by these dogs at home. The fearful dogs are confused as to what is expected, and are trying to avoid haphazard punishment. This dog's owner is often yelling commands loudly and repeatedly, causing the puppy to withdraw from this unpleasantness. A happy dog is often corrected in just as vigorous a manner but he seems to understand why the correction was delivered. Here we have the "heart" of successful dog training—the application of correction without causing confusion and subsequent submission.

The focus of confidence and trainability conditioning is reduction of "submissive" behavior. Submission is displayed in dogs through their posturing. They reduce the physical space they occupy by slinking. Additionally they can show pack signals such as squatting and urinating in the presence of a powerful intruder. In males this submissive urinating is quite different from leg lifting and marking. A dominant dog has convinced the submissive dog, either by prior actions or present behavior, that he should not seek a confrontation but should retreat. In training, a dog that responds submissively to you is being ruined as a protective companion.

In the wild the most obvious submissive display is when a dog lies on his back and urinates as the dominant dog stands above him. Examples of this submission in a training situation include:

1) A dog that grovels at his trainer's feet;
2) A dog who drags or even turns upside down at the end of the leash during the lead breaking process;
3) A dog that upon being scolded grovels and rolls on the ground;
4) A dog that refuses to make eye contact with his owner.

Dogs NATURALLY react to a correction by saluting the authority— bowing to his king—submission, NOT by learning. Submission is a required reaction for the pack animal. The non-submissive dog would be killed by a dominant pack member. Submission is rarely the desired result of correction by a knowledgeable trainer. You, the trainer, are faced with the task of teaching the puppy to perform accurately, consistently, and with zest and enthusiasm—without submission.

What Age To Start?

Training should begin as soon as you obtain your puppy. The sooner the better. Training at this very impressionable age is really guided development rather than teaching tricks or obedience routines. Tricks and obedience routines will come at their proper time, but just as a building requires planning and then beginning from the ground up we must wait to put the windows and roof on only after we have created the basic structure. For this reason, the puppy should be removed from the litter immediately after weaning. This seemingly barbaric act will prevent litter generated submission, and create human rather than dog orientation for the young animal.

We constantly find people who have purchased a puppy through the mail and despite proven excellence in the puppy's parents the puppy is totally inept at learning and fearful of human interaction. In these situations the puppy almost always has been left with his littermates up to the age of fourteen or more weeks. An incredible example of this situation was a puppy that we received from Germany. The pup's sire was the Bundessieger (top working dog in Germany) and his dam (mother) was the only female to reach the working dog championship competition against nineteen males. We expected that the puppy would be bright, energetic, and extremely confident. Our expectations were not fulfilled. He was fearful, submissive, and withdrawn. He sought to avoid human contact and could not even be coaxed into chasing a ball or seeking food treats.

This dog so surprised us that we investigated other animals from the same litter which had been purchased in Germany. None of them had experienced this problem. Our puppy, unlike theirs, was left in a kennel situation among older dogs for many weeks with little human contact. Though he was ready to live a "doggie life" he was ill prepared for human life. No matter how well bred the puppy is, he will not become the dog you want without proper human socialization and a proper early environment.

Prolonged interaction with litter mates (beyond six weeks) allows the litter to become a mini-pack complete with dominant and submissive members. This canine pecking order can only serve to hinder the development of confidence in our potential canine companion's future interaction with human beings. As the litter ages together they become "dog oriented" which simply means that they discover their best friends and playmates, as well as their enemies to be other dogs.

120

This Bulldog loves to "protect" his family.

In some cases, if exposed to the dam of the litter for an excessive period of time they will become fearful of their own mother, as well as other grown dogs. Dog orientation fosters dog aggression, and submission to humans.

The puppy removed from the litter has a new universe. YOU, as the puppy's trainer, will be the center of that universe and become the favorite playmate, mother, father, best friend, sun, moon, and all the planets.

Puppies, Children, and Training At Home

Now that you have the cute little guy it is time to get serious. Plan your program. Set aside DEFINITE TIMES for play periods. Know exactly what you plan to do in each period and why. Don't be lazy. The kids want a playmate, and their attraction to the young puppy is so natural that denying or impeding it would seem to be out of the realm of common sense. However, common sense is really not so common and cannot be expected from the interspecies play of young animals—human or otherwise. Unsupervised play by children negates your control of what the young dog will learn. This is not to say that a child cannot play with the puppy, but rather their play does not fit in with developing a protective dog. Little children frequently do not know their own strength or dominance and can quickly extinguish the spark of confidence in a puppy and sometimes, probably unknowingly, do the puppy physical harm. This obviously depends upon the age of the child and the child's temperament. One of us has an eight year old son whose entire life has involved living with dogs that are assertive, strong, and aggressive. When this boy is bitten by a playful puppy he often responds by either roughly pulling him off or punching him. This works fine in our house where the puppies and the boys live under the supervision of parents well versed in dog training. His friends do not act as he does and will often be frantic in their attempt to fight off or escape a young puppy. One of them struck a young puppy with a heavy metal toy truck when the pup playfully nipped him. This act which horrified our son brought home the importance of supervision and education of children living with dogs.

The converse situation can also occur. A young puppy from aggressive and energetic parents can dominate, frighten, and injure a child. A nine week old puppy which we sold to a family with a one year old daughter has become a terrible problem. This young puppy was introduced into the home with the toddler. The puppy was allowed to play with the child in an unsupervised atmosphere. Soon the puppy realized he was quicker, stronger, and more mobile than the child. In their games the child was a wonderful playmate for the dog. The puppy soon began to nip, chase, knock down and pull the diapers from the child. The parents, expectedly, were disappointed with the puppy and we had to explain to the parents that the puppy's problem was because of their lack of supervision. Once they realized they had to assume responsibility for raising both the child and the puppy the problem was solved. During supervised play they would correct the puppy when he became too aggressive for the child and the child stopped running and screaming at the approach of the puppy.

Children should only interact with a puppy during these early months under your careful supervision until you feel you can trust the relationship.

Games and Confidence for Puppies

Your puppy's attitude to the world can be shaped by games that you play with him. The victory of physical contact and the limits of its

122

authority can be taught in a game. Game playing is actually the earliest form of training. The attitude and rapport that develops during this play period is the foundation for your later serious training.

You should play games that are natural for the puppy—such as tug-of-war with a burlap sack. We find it curious that other schools of training have suggested that this type of play is to be avoided. It is their concern that pulling and tugging will make the puppy aggressive and even dangerous as an adult. We have found the opposite to be true. The game tug-of-war does not make a dog vicious any more than chasing a rolling ball, or stealing a sock.

How the game is played is more important than what the game is. When playing games with your puppy you, as the trainer, must always retain an element of control. For example, when teaching the dog to retrieve, it is helpful if retrieval development was begun with the puppy on a line. In this puppy game capture of the ball is gently but persistently associated with returning it because the line prevents the puppy from learning to do anything other than to bring the object back. Similarly, the tug-of-war will end when the puppy wins. He learns that holding on against resistance is fun until the trainer wants the object released. Only the object (burlap sack) is permitted to be bitten. Anything else such as biting the hand or the person will be corrected. In this game, the puppy will be made to let go of the object on command by saying the word "out" while pressing his lips firmly against his teeth causing significant discomfort. You will very quickly find that only the word "out" will be necessary. Confidence in the game and understanding how the game will end is soon learned by your young dog.

In some situations training must be performed so the dog not only obeys when near his handler but also at great distances or even when his handler is out of sight. This independent canine behavior is learned by using a planned and guided training routine beginning when the dog is a puppy. The dog that will protect, and be confident to act when he hears a command given at a distance is the product of confidence building during his socialization and puppy training. In Europe where the breeding and training of "useful" dogs is a primary goal, there has been developed a specific test to evaluate this aspect of dog behavior/training. The dog and handler are separated on a field after the dog has been placed in a down stay position, the handler is hidden while obvious distractions including other dogs and other trainers are brought within feet of the dog on stay. Without being able to see or hear his trainer for reinforcement the dog must continue to obey though he is receiving no reassurance or approval.

The ability to obey when no longer in sight of the handler is made even more difficult during the next level of testing. An aggressor (in fully padded, protective gear) threatens the dog and his owner at a distance of one hundred feet. The dog must remain under control until the owner gives him a command to meet the aggressor who is now retreating from the dog and the owner. The dog initially pursues the aggressor because of his natural drive to chase an escaping subject. The assailant then turns and runs toward the charging dog. Now the dog must overcome a natural instinct to withdraw or at least stop because he has been trained to continue obeying his original command to meet the assailant whether retreating or running forward. The final portion of the test requires the dog to break the attack upon hearing a single word given by his trainer although he is unable to see where his trainer is calling from.

Puppies that develop into dogs such as these require in their early upbringing the greatest attention to the development of outgoing, confident behavior. This wonderfully confident, robust and self assured puppy can also be a real pain to live with. He is not a cuddly pet. He can often be found nipping rambunctiously, barking assertively, and generally trying to be pushy and important. At this very young age he is trying to control his environment. The extremely confident puppy, developed by these routines, will require a great deal of our energy to control. He **must** have formal obedience training beginning before he is four months of age.

The difference in raising puppies to become different kinds of dogs, is in emphasis rather than method. The emphasis is placed on the degree of outgoing attitude and later aggression which can stem from the puppy's success at dominating his early life experiences. The puppy that has never lost a tug-of-war game is very unlikely as an adult dog to be intimidated by someone other than the trainer in letting go of anything that he has decided to seize. We do not all want an animal that is this headstrong. The same puppy if not consistently allowed to win will be less confident as an adult. This dog is likely to be intimidated by a command shouted at him by a stranger. The confident dog would simply ignore the stranger's order in this same circumstance.

An experienced trainer knows specifically the type of animal he wishes to develop. He will have in his mind a blueprint for choosing the kind of material he wishes to work with and how it should be molded. For example, at the present time the Golden Retriever and Sheltie dominate American Kennel Club obedience rings but they have not competed successfully in sports which require dogs to act forcefully. The success of these breeds in obedience competition is not a fad, fluke, or matter of happenstance, but rather derives from a successful melding of retrieving instincts, sensitivity to correction, and relatively less inclination for dominance than breeds of dogs which will be required to protect or compete in sports requiring strong aggressive traits. These sports are still quite uncommon in the United States, and therefore dogs that have been bred for them are in a distinct minority. This situation is not the same in Europe where the testing and competition of dogs is directed toward strength in aggressive and protective characteristics. For this reason these animals are not better than dogs that are inclined to be less aggressive but have been molded for a different purpose. These dogs must be capable of the quickness to obey as in our own obedience trials, and yet able to deal with an aggressor.

After recognition of the dog's individual character as defined by his breed, and more immediately his line of breeding, we can control his upbringing to create a close approximation of our ideal.

We acknowledge that there are limits to training, and we do not seek the impossible. The impossible is trying to make a man-stopper from a toy breed, or an acrobatic obedience animal from one of the giant breeds. No matter what the training goal is, it will be accomplished by stressing aspects common to all training. Where we place this emphasis is the way we recognize the differences between our breeds.

We place strong emphasis on confidence building for the future protection dog who will later be required to act independently and aggressively with discretion. The obedience oriented trainer will also require confidence from his dog, but emphasis here will be upon compliance to command, with a happy and willing attitude. For these dogs independent and dominant behavior will not be required in later life and consequently will not be emphasized in this early upbringing. This permits development of a more compliant dog. It is for this reason our program for raising a puppy will be contingent upon its ultimate goal.

A toy such as the "puppy tug" can achieve the same important response in young dogs and yet will eventually have different purposes for different dogs in their adult life. The future competitive obedience dog or the future home protector both should be started with this toy. The "puppy tug" toy is a soft roll of burlap with a leather handle on one or both ends. The puppy's natural instinct is to grab at the tug and try to steal it from the human. This leads to the natural development of a tug-of-war game.

The tug-of-war game instills confidence in the young dog without causing submission. The puppy becomes comfortable with a person roughhousing with him in close proximity. The trainer in this situation develops the ability to control the puppy by instituting or ending the game as desired. The puppy anticipates and responds with enthusiasm to the trainer and the recognition of his toy.

This toy will help develop a confident young animal that will show vigor and enthusiasm when trained for such diverse roles as retrieving or protecting. The dog trained with an emphasis for obedience will benefit from early roughhousing and using the tug toy by developing enthusiasm for entering into new experiences which can be translated later into passion for retrieval and jumping. This zest for training does not mean that your advanced obedience dog (Utility Dog) will be running out of control and refuse to release the objects retrieved. Instead, it means that he will not slink over to the jump and stand there, tail between his legs, when commanded to retrieve.

Despite our best intentions and sincere efforts in training our young dog, we must be candid with ourselves about poor results. If our attempts at conditioning our puppy to strange noises, winning tug-of-war games, running after a ball, and prey chasing are consistently met with failure then perhaps we have chosen the wrong puppy. Be honest with yourself because it still is not too late to choose a different puppy. If you have a strong desire to compete in the training sports rather than having a dog that will only be "a loving pet" then maybe you need another start. Puppies are the hardest things in the world to return because of our rapid emotional bonding with them, but we must remind ourselves that it is unfair to the puppy to raise him in an environment which will make demands upon him that are not within his genetic potential. Nor should we try to work with anything less than the best when we are committing to a three to five year investment in our training program.

Behavior Modification

The sensitive, pack-oriented canine animal is trained by the other animals with which he lives. The very young puppy, be he wolf or dog, has his first weeks of development well structured by his mother and his later development by the other members of the pack. In the case of the domesticated puppy we are introducing ourselves near the end of what would be his mother/puppy relationship. For this reason the responsibility then falls upon us to direct his early life. We will teach him patterns of behavior which should be well thought out and carefully planned. In this way we may avoid having the dog learn destructive behavior, and permit him to obtain gratification by pleasing us. We will do this as the wild family does, by correcting antisocial behavior and rewarding desirable behavior. The pleasure-principle of reward has been called by some "inductive training." Regardless of the name we attach to it, we seek to motivate our puppy by providing him with rewards and a sense of well being. Whether this is the mother's warmth, cleaning of his coat by other pack members, or our petting and proffering food, the result is the same. Appropriate behavior brings reward and pleasure. When the puppy performs inappropriately, the mother dog grabs him by the scruff of the neck, knocks him over, and performs other physical corrections. So also do we make corrections—called by some "compulsive" behavior modification. The differences between these two techniques are profound, and the art of dog training is their proper mixture. The reward principal will create drive, enthusiasm, and confidence, but does not always assure consistency of behavior. The correction by a noxious stimulus, such as a collar jerk or the mother's grabbing of the scruff of the neck extinguishes behavior, and if ill-applied will diminish enthusiasm and can make a consistent animal but one who is sad and "hang dog" in appearance.

We will list some methods of behavior modification which will lead to an economy of time used in training, provide an appropriate environment prior to and during training, and describe some of the potential pitfalls you may encounter in using these techniques.

Compulsive Training

Compulsive training is one of the most misunderstood aspects of raising a puppy and later in training the dog. Nothing could be more

UNNATURAL than for a puppy to be raised in a world where he receives no corrections, learns no limits, and never has unruly or destructive behavior corrected. Many of us, because of our reluctance to inflict pain, suffer the same problems when raising children. Correcting or punishing is a negative action for both the puppy and the trainer. Since it is so much easier to reward, we can fall into the trap of trying to cajole, seduce, or distract our puppy out of his negative behavior. This technique will not work with a puppy any more than with children. In the beginning we must say NO, not just with our voice, but with physical emphasis. The mother wolf or dog emitting a low growl with her physical correction on the puppy's neck can eventually obtain the same results with only the growl and no longer needs to administer the physical correction. Similarly, we will eventually reach a point where the sound of our voice saying, "NO," carries with it the implied physical correction and therefore will bring prompt results. Errors in training, however, usually stem from not making this association firm and lasting. Too early use of an indecisive verbal NO may plant the seeds of delayed obedience and later flagrant disobedience. It is far kinder to correct the still sensitive puppy than to have to resort to stronger correction with the larger adult dog. We have observed that consistent and properly-timed use of puppy corrections tremendously lessens both the intensity and frequency of correction needed in the adult dog. Thus, for us, compulsive training, (training with the avoidance of discomfort as a psychological basis) is mandatory and no matter how liberal or kind we are, we must recognize the ultimate disservice to the dog when this training is not applied during his formative months.

Prior to weaning, the puppy has been exposed to very little negative reinforcement from people. His mother has begun this training and when the puppy has been made our charge we must continue it. The need will become more evident as our confidence-building techniques bear fruit.

This early conditioning has now prepared the puppy for training which will use both positive and negative reinforcement. "Compulsive training" is a method which is only successful when used in combination with reward. Reward—or positive reinforcement training—is frequently called "inductive training." Neither of these systems can, of themselves, serve to train a dog. If there is art as well as science in dog training, then it is in being able to mix the proper blend of these ingredients for our successful recipe. For this kind of "cookbook training," the recipe will need to be varied according to the genetic behavioral characteristics of the dog with whom we are working.

Our mixing of the reward system of training with the compulsive system has permitted confidence and trainability. This allows the animal to receive a correction, "negative reinforcement" without cowering. It allows the puppy to be subordinate to the trainer yet be very confident. The puppy who has had this confidence instilled does not become suspicious of our actions after a correction, nor does he become sulky and refuse to work. He remains enthusiastic, continuing his training as a happy worker. The correction is therefore limited by the response it evokes from the puppy. This limitation means that he has "learned how to learn," that a correction is not a preamble to continued abuse. For this reason, he does not need to submit or assume a frightened posture so as to ward off successive corrections. This is no longer a dominance versus submission interaction between trainer and dog, but rather what could be called a natural correction. Just as touching a hot stove causes one not to repeat this activity, so should the natural correction. This is the difference between correction and punishment. Punishment implies mental anguish and anticipation of discomfort. This anticipation can cause submission in the puppy in an attempt to prevent further discomfort. Natural correction, not associated with a human being is limited to stopping behavior without damaging the psyche because the trainer of the puppy did not cause his "hurt." So in its purest form the puppy's action caused him to be "hurt" while the trainer appeared to be an INNOCENT BYSTANDER.

We can now generalize that the goal of compulsive training is not to create submission or even to permit it. Compulsive training, when built upon a foundation of reward generated confidence-raising, is exceedingly limited—as are the corrections in the wild. To pursue this, we have used such techniques as administering a collar tug from a hand not seen by the dog, thus changing what would appear to the dog to be a classic trainer-administered correction to a natural one. "Where did that collar jerk come from?" wonders the dog. For the very young puppy then, a collar jerk should be administered when he is looking away, particularly if he is ignoring you when you call his name. Again, the art of dog training is being able to pay enough attention to the puppy, where he is looking, how he is responding to your voice, and being determined enough to get the timing right. Correct timing—jerking the collar quickly and sharply and yet not allowing the puppy (by your body postures or tone of voice) to think the correction came from you. Thus, this natural correction often is as difficult to accomplish as it is effective. It is so much easier for us to harp at the puppy, give repetitive nagging corrections, or become angry, all of which will guarantee two counterproductive responses: 1) The puppy will associate the correction with us. 2) He may then create a submissive posturing and withdraw from the entire training activity.

Administering the "natural correction" is an athletic accomplishment. It must be worked at and honed, just as we would in the development of an effective tennis serve. The only thing natural about it is that the puppy does not know its origin, but for us it is quite unnatural as it requires, just as the tennis serve, careful attention, coordination, and most of all, self control.

There are certain spirited puppies who have so flourished under our confidence-development that the first "handler" correction for them may provoke confrontation. Handler correction, as distinguished from the natural correction, means that the puppy knows that it was YOU who has administered this negative reinforcement. This is a critical time which must be handled with firmness, but firmness that is so modulated as to not allow you to finally win at the cost of abject submission by the dog.

Our conditioned puppy may become argumentative because our attempt to make him confident may have outweighed our attempt to set limits. This is always a problem since individual dogs vary so much that what would have been a correction to be avoided in one dog may have been mandatory in another. We can best judge how well we are doing by continuing to observe the puppy's attitude. If he seems to resent correction and behave as if our correction was a challenge, then we have not set proper limits and must do so.

An example of uncontrolled confidence was provided by a young dog I was training. Rather than being submissive this young male was so enthusiastic and fearless that when I began obedience training and made a sharp correction the dog ripped the sleeve from my new shirt. Clearly I had been successful in avoiding socializing that dampened the dogs spirit or caused submission. The socializing was not balanced. Limits had not been established. Control in this instance meant establishing limits. From the pup's earliest sessions I had avoided correction. Nothing the dog did was ever wrong, so he felt he could do ANYTHING. The most basic correction that was neglected was for me to prohibit his biting me. There is an art to preventing your puppy from biting you without extinguishing all aggressive behavior. This is accomplished by "bite transference." The dogs aggression is displaced by permitting him to bite something like the puppy tug.

In training a protective dog, balance is the key. Confidence and aggression must be tempered with control. Neither can go unchecked. Confidence developed without control creates a lack of respect for the human—potentially a dangerous circumstance. Control and correction without the ability of the dog to transfer his aggression creates submission. Thus it is wise during a difficult training session to interrupt the session with rough and vigorous play. The dog is not beaten down by repetitive obedience corrections and he is shown that acting vigorously is tolerated and even encouraged. Our training provides an escape mechanism for the dog's pent-up frustration.

We have found it necessary to intersperse positive reinforcement, such as praise followed by food reward, to maintain our bond with the dog and not allow ourselves to be viewed only as his tormentor. The person who corrects his dog without adequate re-establishment of the animals trust will defeat his own purpose. The dog will cease to learn and seek only to avoid and flee. Learning cannot be effective when correction and praise are not in harmony. When correction is misunderstood by the dog he learns avoidance ploys. An extreme example of this, that we have witnessed, is frequently caused with the use of the electric collar. A dog shocked while digging in one part of the backyard will stay away from that part of the yard, but may continue to dig in another. Then when the dog is shocked in the new location while digging the dog avoids this area as well. All too often this training will continue until the dog no longer goes into the backyard. This is avoidance!

The first correction that a dog understands as originating from the handler will be a most important test. The training must be firm, and the handler must make the dog appreciate that he will not be able to yowl himself out of the correction. Yet it must not be so heavy handed as to cause him lasting fear. The trainer should remember the difference between correction and punishment/abuse which teaches avoidance.

The training methods that we have discussed include reward and punishment or positive and negative reinforcement. These concepts are as old as the first glimmers of our attempts to understand human or animal learning. It is their application and mixture which so often eludes us and hinders us from developing the dog that we really want.

A major problem is our desire to talk to and try to explain to the dog what we want him to do. This is a basic mistake that derives from applying what we know of the human world to the dog. Our natural dependence on verbal communication when dealing with our dog is both pathetic and humorous. The well-intentioned trainer trying to "talk" his dog out of doing something fails no matter how reasonable his argument or seductive his reward. It just never works! This same person would not approach an inhabitant of remote Finland and expect an appropriate response to his well structured English speech, yet for some reason he thinks that his dog will somehow understand the logic and fairness of his verbal request.

Another failing, in our transition from the human to the canine world, is our overestimation of the dog's ability to understand cause and effect. We are all so sophisticated that it does not occur to us that we could administer a correction and the dog not know where it originated. However this is quite common with the dog particularly during the early months of his life when training can very effectively use natural correction. If the dog does not see you making the correction the dog will presume the correction originated from his behavior—not yours. These two failings illustrate much of what we need to overcome in our own attitudes when attempting to raise and train dogs. We want our canine friends to be objects of our "love." Consequently we will falsely identify them with having human characteristics and this impedes the training process severely. These characteristics which we confer upon our canine trainees are:

1) The ability to understand language in sentence form.

2) A level of canine understanding which would, if present, allow them to "catch on" to the natural correction and not permit its success.

We must continually do battle against our feelings which make little furry people out of our dogs (anthropomorphism). Who has not laughed at the dog wearing a man's hat? Though it is cute, it denigrates the dog's canine identity and creates the weakest possible basis for his training. Our love for them, makes us assume levels of sophistication they do not have. This leads to our disappointment over their inability to understand the spoken word. Thus, we set unrealistic goals and create training techniques which include much verbalization and little instant reward or punishment. Then we wonder why they do not learn. Frequently, this is the basis for the development of human frustration which, in so many situations, is vented upon the dog as undeserved anger. And, of course, the anger further diminishes the animal's receptivity to learning. When there is a problem, it is OUR problem, not the dog's. He should not feel guilty, disappointed, or frustrated, for these feelings are our projections which we have put upon him. He will begin almost as a blank page for us to write our instructions and it is incumbent upon us to make these instructions simple, repetitive, and clear.

BIG GUY, LITTLE GUY

FUN AND GAMES

Puppy Prep-School

Just as doting parents spend a great deal of their time and resources trying to get the best from their children, so can we, as puppy owners, work to get the best from our dogs. We can have our home serve as the young dog's preschool. As wise Headmasters we will keep things interesting, fun, and yet always be aware of our educational goal and the discipline and attention to detail that will be required to accomplish it. The education of young puppies has similarities to the education of young children. We will be limited by the short attention span of our student, restless behavior and distractibility. For these reasons "games" will continue to be used for educational purposes and recreation in a more sophisticated manner.

In order to train our puppy during his tender months, games serve as an invaluable aid. Practicing these games will permit us to hone the temperament of our future dog. Specifically the game plan listed below will help achieve the basic behavior orientation of adult dog training. Many of these techniques have been used by the most successful competition dog trainers. Some of the techniques are "tricks of the trade" that will be employed by those who want a zestful, confident, energetic dog. Remember, these methods are not needed in raising a companion dog, foot warmer, or agreeable canine ornament. If you need a dog that you hope will be a "babe in arms," or a pet just to fuss over please don't employ these exercises.

Directed Play

The directed play of the puppy will encourage avoidance of submission, confidence development, and provide an introduction to required later exercises. If we are successful, these exercises will be approached by the dog with enthusiasm and he will not find himself needing to unlearn behaviors which contradict the obedience we seek. We can get a happy and precise working puppy by directing early play to games which will channel his enthusiasm and activities. When these games are fun, so will be the dog's life.

We must however control and direct our puppy's time. To do this, he should be kept in a dog crate or backyard pen, and taken out to play and exercise with his trainer. Our rule is that the puppy is free only when we are present to supervise. The puppy should never be allowed to roam the house alone, or even worse, should never be allowed to roam free in the neighborhood. Both his safety and learning will suffer and if he survives you may have a canine Godzilla on your hands.

It is a fallacy to believe that your puppy requires the company of other dogs. This is not so—because he now belongs to a human pack. Other dogs are unfair competition for YOU as the trainer. Quite naturally they will have more in common with your dog and teach him to behave as they do, NOT in the manner your training prescribes. Don't get a pet for your pet! Even your canine obedience champion will not teach your puppy to "heel" or "down" on command.

You are not raising a "show dog" or a friendly pet. You are training a pet/protector! You don't want your puppy to spend his whole life in that crate or in a dog run! We hasten to remind you that the training period from six weeks to six months will develop the temperament and disposition with which you must live for years to come. The unsupervised puppy, left to his own devices, will quickly learn such habits and behavior as how to eat the couch, how to shred drapery, how to remove carpet, etc. The first question you must answer is fundamental—do you want to train the puppy or are you going to permit him to train you? One of our clients made an astute observation, "The more I supervise the puppy the less I need to watch the dog." Containment and supervision of the puppy leads to more freedom and less need for supervision of the mature animal.

The trainer should be jealous of the puppy's time, allowing the puppy to play only the trainer's games and only when the trainer wants to play! Anything less structured creates the potential opportunity for the dog to develop random habits and patterns of behavior that are counterproductive to patterns which we call training. A puppy that grabs an article and runs from you, forcing you to chase him, is training you. He is also developing a game which will make it more difficult for you to make him reliable in performing the retrieving exercises later in his career. Similarly, a dog which makes a game of your pursuing him is not just playing a harmless game of tag, but creating contradictory patterns to later recall exercises. It is our belief that what are described as unruly dogs have often developed self-injurious habits by participating in unguided or laissez-faire play. Your dog's play needs to be structured. We do not have the luxury, as with our own children, of being able to explain verbally why certain types of behavior were acceptable when they were toddlers are no longer acceptable now that they are in school. Highly structured play is important with young dogs, as opposed to young children, because we can verbally "undo" the child's unacceptable behavior, but rigorous, correction laden training will be required to undo what we did not correctly teach the dog in the first place. This not only creates a tremendous loss of time but adds negative and "confidence injuring" corrections which could have been avoided by initial careful attention to the young puppy's play time. Misdirected or unsupervised play is often an excuse for negligence or laziness of the trainer.

Energy Direction

We must keep the puppy interested in playing with us. This will initially be an easy task, but 'familiarity breeds contempt' and overexposure to the trainer breeds indifference. A dog must be paying attention to his trainer to learn anything. The pup that pays attention means that the trainer continues to be interesting to the puppy and is not taken for granted. Instead, the puppy eagerly anticipates the trainer's arrival to break the boredom of the day. We must be able to compete with whatever the puppy has been doing in our absence. It is much easier get the full attention of the puppy who has been somewhat bored while we were away than to expect to achieve full concentration from a puppy that has been chasing butterflies, unravelling balls of yarn, chewing happily on furniture, and investigating every nook and cranny of your home. When you keep that same puppy safe and secure in a crate and take him out for directed play, he is dynamite. Just as important in maintaining his enthusiasm in directed play is not permitting him to tire, become bored, and wander off somewhere. When his attention slips, stop the play/training and put him away again.

The length of play periods are then determined by the puppy's interest. For instance, if you want to play ball during the training period, then do so only as long as the puppy continues to play. When his interest drifts, then he is returned to the dog crate where he can sleep undisturbed. The result of this energy direction is:

1) The puppy will learn to anticipate play/training time.

2) When he is taken out, the puppy will make the trainer the center of his attention.

3) His activity level is controlled and directed.

4) Training the adult dog will be a natural outgrowth of puppy training.

Raising the puppy in a planned environment and structuring his time with us allows the orderly development of the future family member and protector. He will have had a certain loss of early freedom, but he will gain in the long run by being permitted greater responsibility in terms of being able to live free within our home and be a valued companion rather than a nuisance or problem.

Confidence In The Family Protector "Tug-o-War"

In order for a dog to have the self assurance to stand his ground in the face of a threat or intruder his development requires both nature and nurture. The nature refers to the puppy's inherent drives while his nurture means the way he was raised. The degree of importance that each of these components play is a matter of controversy. Despite the fact that some dogs and breeds are more assertive than others, this characteristic can be enhanced for the home protector by puppy games.

Tug-o-war is a very natural game for the puppy. You need a burlap sack, towel, or just an old rag. Drag the sack along the floor and get the puppy interested. Over a period of time his interest will intensify

Increased enthusiasm is accomplished by spirited games. Tug-o-War is a favorite.

and he will become aggressive toward the tug-toy. The game must end with the puppy winning—getting the object. After several such sessions, the puppy will become increasingly confident that he can steal the sack from you. As this begins to happen, you should make it increasingly more difficult for him to win. You might even develop a "bark on command," using the puppy's frustration for the tug toy as a stimulus. This game will not make your puppy grow into a snarling man-eater. This play has made him confident and more likely to look upon the world with self assurance. As the puppy grows older the game can be expanded, but this should be done under the supervision of a professional dog trainer.

The professional trainer will be able to explain the meaning of a full bite, and how to teach your dog to release on command without causing the dog to feel he has just done something wrong.

Training beyond the tug-o-war stage requires the owner to make a commitment for extended obedience schooling. This level of canine assertiveness is NOT defensive aggression for the dog. This is still "chase and capture" play but it is teaching the skills which the dog will utilize later in his aggression work. Dogs naturally bite, but often only when unable to escape. This play makes the dog more confident in his interactions reducing his tendency to run from threat.

Since we are seeking a companion and home protector, we must channel his developing self-assertion. The puppy must not be permitted to assert himself in the household. Tugging on the sack is OK but protecting his food by growling, biting the trainer during play, or dominating the children is not acceptable. These are common problems with strong puppies—especially males. The same problem can arise in a household that has done no developmental training with the puppy and has failed to correct these instinctual drives. In cases such as this the dog has trained the owner and then the dog must be removed from the home (usually into the back yard) and finally is put to sleep for "turning" on the owner.

Confidence building also means the trainer controls the game. This is quite different from the home where there has been no training and the dog is permitted to assert himself in an increasingly vigorous fashion. These are the dogs that later have no reason to exercise restraint against doing injury to get their way. They have not learned to be a protective member of their human family, are useless—and dangerous. The protective dog respects his home, and is confident within himself to stand his ground.

Retrieval

Retrieval is not usually thought to be a part of training a protective dog. This skill however incorporates guiding the prey-drive of the dog into a consistent behavior pattern. Chasing a ball—or any object thrown—is a natural instinct of the animal. Bringing the object back to his handler is not. For this retrieval to be CONSISTENTLY performed the dog must be trained to suppress his natural instinct to run away and enjoy what he has captured. Teaching this routine permits the dog to learn that 'capture' does not equal 'possession.' The dog, while very enthusiastic, still is required to obey. In advanced protection work, where the dog seizes a padded sleeve while in an excited state, he must also learn to release upon command. In both situations the dog begins an act—capture of the man or ball—in a state of excitement but returns to a state of control by voice command.

Generally speaking, a ball is the best retrieval object. The more lively the ball the better. A worn tennis ball makes an excellent toy for a young dog. The prey-chasing instinct that most puppies possess will usually be sparked by a rolling ball. Keep your training/play sessions short. Be sure not to extend the playtime beyond the puppy's interest and take the ball away after the game is over. Do not let the puppy use it as a chew toy.

Trainer frustration is common when the puppy does not seem interested in retrieving. This trainer usually sees the problem as, "My puppy cannot learn to retrieve. I have tried everything and nothing works." As a matter of fact, All dogs (not mentally retarded) can be taught to retrieve IF the trainer has enough patience. As in other training, retrieval takes time—much more time than an average trainer will willingly tolerate.Confine the puppy except for playing with a ball. Spend two or three minutes several times daily attempting to play with the ball. This always works, but it COULD take several weeks, even months. (My dog took over four months to learn to retrieve, now it is his obsession.)

One extremely good method of creating interest in the ball is to tie the puppy on a three-foot line along a wall. Then you move eight or ten feet away from the wall and dog and bounce the ball against the wall in a keep-away fashion. The game for you is to see how close to the puppy you can bounce the ball. The game for the puppy is to "steal" the ball. When the puppy gets the ball then praise and play with the puppy while he holds the ball. If the puppy drops the ball steal it back and resume the game.

140

Never allow the puppy to keep the ball when the games are over. The ball must be special and important for him to possess. It is always associated with the trainer and should never become an idle chew toy.

Rough Play and Channeling Aggression

An important part of a puppies growth is the experience he receives when he is first touched by people. His understanding of what to expect is imprinted from these early experiences. The importance of touch learning cannot be overemphasized.

Within the litter puppies soon learn the difference between play and biting that is too painful to be permitted. As puppies tussle in an attempt to dominate each other they will nip with increasing intensity. Their bite will increase until the other puppy responds by biting back

Learning the biting game of "prey" drive.

Pup not only grabs sleeve but attempts to pull it from agitator.

Pup is shown by a skilled agitator that he should fear nothing—not even a stick.

Confident pup holds on while being lifted from ground.

harder. This interaction teaches them the control of their bite as well as the limits of their authority.

This natural regulation of the bite and limitation of authority is often difficult for people to imitate. The two errors that are commonly made are at the extremes of human behavior, passivity, or domination of the puppy. Those that interact with the puppy by not responding to his increasing assertiveness, and allowing him to become ever more forceful in his play assume the risk of creating a dog who will bite them.

The other problem occurs for the opposite reason. The trainer teaches the puppy fear of human interaction because he has been frightened. Human overreaction, usually an anger response, will create fear, avoidance and submission in the puppy. Therefore the perfect puppy development will require careful modulating of our tolerance of his behavior with control that will teach him limits but not submission. We have found that play, including a gradual escalation of the roughness of that play will accomplish this purpose. It also will permit the careful trainer to increase or limit the eventual level of aggressiveness that the mature dog will develop.

We begin by simply handling the puppy—rolling him off of his feet, and stroking him with our fingers. Some puppies, six to eight weeks old, will respond by grabbing at our hands and/or growling while trying to regain their balance. This is the beginning of a game that allows the puppy to realize that when pushed or touched he will not be hurt and he can respond by pushing back and using his mouth. After the puppy demonstrates a clear pattern of behavior so that pushing and playing with him makes him respond by using his mouth, we then channel this response. Redirecting the puppy from our hands to a toy is the next building block of the game. As the puppy grabs for us he is given the opportunity to bite a piece of towel, rubber ring, or other suitable bite/pull toy. The puppy quickly makes this transfer and eagerly looks forward to playing the game.

The transfer to the toy is called channeling and allows us, as the puppy gets older and stronger, to increase the vigor of the game. Since his biting does not produce pain for us we can increase the degree of difficulty of the game by pulling harder on the toy. While the puppy is biting on the toy we may stroke him, tap him on the head with our fingers, rub his fur against the grain, and load him with tactile stimuli while he is playing.

The top puppy holds the sleeve hesitantly at its farthest point from the submissive trainer.

Puppy tries to steal burlap with feet, but is intimidated by upright trainer.

Confident puppy bites sleeve and is lifted from the ground by a dominant trainer.

The puppy becomes used to being roughed up but NOT HURT while playing. When the puppy bites us during the game, the game stops. For the puppy the fun happens only when he plays the game the way we want him to play it. In this manner we teach him limits while permitting him to expand his confidence with human touch and interaction.

During his growth, our play with the puppy increases in roughness. Pull the puppy's hair, push, slap, scold (yell), and when he shows aggression, withdraw and give him a bite on the toy. If the puppy withdraws, you have overstepped and are doing something dumb! In the beginning, the puppy is allowed, even encouraged, to focus his aggression on the trainer—but not to actually bite the trainer—and the trainer acts submissive. As conditioning progresses, the trainer does not need to act as submissive as he once did. This puppy will gain confidence and aggression to the degree that he may learn to initiate play himself even within a six week period of training!

When aggression is strong, DISPLACE or CHANNEL the aggression to a burlap sack via the tug-of-war game mentioned above. Roll the sack up and tie a knot in it. When the puppy responds to the rough plan, redirect this aggression by always making the sack available and encourage his fighting with it as if he were making a kill. As the puppy becomes secure with this outlet for his aggression then the fight for the sack can become more vigorous—always the puppy wins and gets the sack. During the fight phase, the trainer should resist by yelling, scolding, slapping, pulling hair, but the puppy ALWAYS wins. Again, the trainer must "read" the puppy for the correct time to back off and show trainer submission.

Positive Reinforcement "Food Craving"

A dog that eagerly accepts food during obedience training is a happy worker. One that won't take treats will be unhappy, unwilling, and a chore to train.

Food is a valuable aid in training. Food is a positive motivation only if the dog is hungry. Feed your puppy on a regular schedule but do not leave food accessible to him all the time. Make eating special. Give the puppy his dinner and then remove the dish after five to ten minutes whether or not he has eaten it. The time span the food is left to be eaten can be gradually reduced to five minutes over a period of weeks.

Provide food treats only when the puppy has performed something worthy of a reward. Call the puppy to you—when he comes praise then treat. Or command him to sit, place him in a sitting position then reward him. Command, "Down," and reward him when he lies down. Our goal is for the puppy to anxiously and aggressively devour a food reward even after *he has received a correction!*

Negative Reinforcement (compulsion again)

Thus far the puppy has been exposed to very little negative reinforcement. Up to this point, we have stopped unwanted behavior by ending the game. When we withdrew our participation, indirect negative reinforcement was achieved. This however will not be sufficient as the puppy becomes more sophisticated and independent. Direct negative reinforcement (compulsive training) will be required to be added to our training technique. This is a turning point after confidence and trainability conditioning has molded the puppy to respond to a negative reinforcement (correction) rather than submitting to it. It is important that this compulsive training be started only after a positive attitude has been cultivated in the puppy by our preceding games, play and rewards.

You can expect resistance when you introduce the compulsive phase of training. Our conditioned puppy is smart, confident and ambitious. He wants to be dominant. He wants to train—not be trained. Frequently a dominance struggle takes place when teaching the compulsive "down." The trainer commands, "Down," and applies a negative motivation using the training collar. In dog language the human is stating, "I am your leader, your superior. You will lie down and show me proper respect when you do." Sometimes the dog growls, shows teeth and replies, "You can't make me lie down." (The down is a submissive posture for the dog.) "I am powerful and will give you a correction with my teeth if you try it." Recently a dog I was training destroyed a new shirt and bit me several times before he finally realized I was the trainer and not he.

I had done my job well and for my purposes he was conditioned against submission, as well as being confident. I was aware that my training had failed to teach the dog limits. The dominance struggle was the result of my permissiveness, not a fault of the dog. I had to remain objective and not lose my temper. Loss of temper by the trainer can destroy the puppy's attitude and risk losing everything for which he has been working. When a trainer loses control, the situation is that of one dumb (but not mute) animal abusing another. To train successfully, one cannot be dumb.

When the puppy has "learned how to learn," then he is ready for serious training. This means that the puppy will accept a negative reinforcement (collar correction) and NOT SUBMIT, but will instead modify his behavior—which is our intention.

A correction by the handler differs from the "automatic" correction. The difference is the puppy's understanding of where the correction comes from. Both corrections cause discomfort, and both are compulsive. But with the automatic correction the dog learns in the absence of the trainer. The dog believes the discomfort originates from his own action. If the dog KNOWS a correction has been administered by the trainer, then it is a "handler" correction. A correction to maintain a sit-stay, correct for a wide about turn, or a correction to teach the down command are all examples of handler corrections. In contrast, the puppy DOESN'T KNOW where an "automatic" correction has come from. This distinction is important, as the automatic correction will not induce submissive behavior.

Examples of the automatic correction can be found with the proper use of an electric collar correction or a throw chain correction. If the dog sees you throwing a chain, then you have made a handler correction, not an automatic correction. The purpose of the automatic correction is to allow the "smart" trainer to make corrections without the implications of the handler-given correction. Thus, automatic corrections can be applied while the puppy is still naive, before the puppy is ready for the compulsive phase.

Be careful when you administer handler corrections to a submissive puppy. If submission persists, then the majority of corrections should be automatic. Handler corrections are necessary to establish respect for the trainer in a confident dog, but can be risky while working with a submissive one. Handler corrections enable the confident puppy to recognize limits. Eventually all dogs must accept handler corrections. Regular obedience exercises are taught with handler corrections.

The trainer must maintain a balance between the dog's desire to act and the correction required to direct that action. The dog that shows this happy attitude THINKS he is getting his way. The problem is how to make your puppy THINK he wants to lie down, think he wants to get that dumbbell, and convince himself that he prefers "heel position."

Agility, strength, and obedience all tested in Schutzhund exercises.

Attention is essential for obedience training. Dog's gaze tells the whole story.

Obedience

Training a dog to understand our wishes, and then follow our commands is the goal of obedience training. Obedience is the language between dogs and people. It is our most effective way to communicate. Vocabulary used in dog training is phonetic and involves twenty or fewer commands. This is all that most dogs are able to respond to and comprehend. Translating the words of our language to sounds understandable to the dog is the heart of obedience training. Some training such as housebreaking and keeping off the furniture, requires only that the dog respond to the command, "NO."

The alternative to training your dog is having your dog train you! In a man/dog relationship training is always going on for one or the other. Dog obedience training reinforces the fact to the dog that you are the teacher and he is the student. It is surprising how many dog owners are unaware of this and allow themselves to become students to their dog's instruction. The dog's commands are simple such as, "Don't bother me while I'm eating," "I'll sleep where I want," "It may be your shoe, but it's MY toy!" Since these commands are direct, the dog will train you to obey them quickly using his compulsive methods such as growling (the word no), giving a deaf ear to your commands, or biting (the dog's punishment when you don't listen). Dogs are excellent teachers since they do not hedge their commands, nor worry about whether they are liked. Guilt, as far as we know, does not prevent them from making a correction nor from seeing their desires as more urgent than yours. Dog obedience courses then become a refuge for all of us indecisive, caring, and somewhat guilt-ridden humans.

Dog training is something that must be learned from doing. Since the exercises the dog must learn are so simple for us it would appear that teaching them also appears simple. It is for this reason that so many "how-to" books are written and yet so few dogs are adequately trained. Teaching a dog is not simple or easy and will require professional assistance.

This instruction can be either the salvation or the ruin of the future man/dog relationship. The dog owners arrive for the first session of the obedience course with no idea of what to expect from themselves, their dog or their trainer. They find themselves suddenly in a "classroom" with ten to fifteen other equally nervous owners and dogs. All may end well if this class is directed by a patient, experienced and expert teacher. Sadly this is not very often the case. The bad experiences so frequently encountered in classes conducted by mediocre trainers CAN be avoided by beginning preschool at home. Training of your dog should begin from the moment the pup is handed over to you and carried on continuously long before coming to class. Thus the obedience that is described below is a continuation in more formal ways, of the training that begins with game playing.

The methods of raising a puppy to this point in time should have produced an attitude which is responsive to direction and training. Your dog will not be one that recognizes clues such as when he has his collar on it is time to obey. Your voice and demeanor will be the source of his stimulus for training. This is the more natural type of behavior for a dog, as he is a pack animal and oriented to carefully examining the attitudes and postures of other members in his pack (your family).

You have avoided the pitfall of giving signals that this is his training time by speaking to him in the same tone of voice whether he is being trained or not. Also, he wears his collar and sometimes may even drag a lead while he is at home. Thus training is incorporated into his daily living and it takes only little effort for you to reach down and enforce your verbal command by a tug on the lead or collar.

When you first purchase your dog's collar, let the dog wear it for a day or so undisturbed. This way he will become so used to it that it will no longer be an object separate from his body. Then, attach a leash and let the dog drag the leash around the house for another day. The leash is now something new, and again there will need to be a period of accommodation. When you observe that the dog is now bored with and ignoring the lead you may begin training. A word of caution is needed, particularly with young dogs. The lead should be on the 'dead ring' or on a non-choke collar to avoid any mishap if the leash becomes snagged when the dog is out of your sight.

Now, you are ready to begin training. Your first move is to make yourself the object of the dog's attention. This fundamental practice cannot be overestimated in value. We have witnessed hundreds of otherwise intelligent people trying their hardest to train a dog who was just plain ignoring them. People who have quite successfully performed obedience routines with a dog in their home or yard suddenly, when in public, find the dog acting as if he has previously learned nothing at all. The problem here is the distraction of the new environment. For this reason all successful trainers are aware that the dog's attention must be focused on them regardless of where they are. Thus training amid distractions becomes the most successful way to insure consistency in the dog's behavior.

How do you know if your dog is paying attention to you? Very few dogs that we have met have proven to be great philosophic thinkers, gazing at the sky or at another dog as they think great thoughts. Trust me—IF YOUR DOG IS NOT LOOKING AT YOU HE IS NOT PAYING ATTENTION TO YOU! Thus it is mandatory for you as a successful trainer to work hard in paying attention to where your dog is looking. If you do not do this your efforts to train your dog will fail—guaranteed. We have seen thousands of humorous results when trainer and dog gaze off in different directions.

If your dog is staring at another dog in dog language he is calling the other dog bad names. The other dog stares back and they engage in a name calling battle. If the two dogs are able to physically reach each other, a physical confrontation (dog fight) will take place. The purpose is to see who has the right to say bad things to whom—or maybe who gets to kill whom.

If you are the boss your dog MUST give you his full attention. There are two fundamental methods to achieve this. One is based on positive motivation. He will look at you constantly in anticipation of something good happening. This good thing can be a food treat that is presented to him at random intervals or after he has responded properly to an obedience command. Other types of good things can be something FUN that the dog can anticipate happening such as getting to chase a ball or stick. These techniques, since they produce good feelings and happy anticipation, are described as 'positive reinforcement.' The type of training that utilizes **only** positive reinforcement is described by some as inductive training.

The second method of obtaining your dog's attention is by correction. This means that the dog experiences something unpleasant when he is not paying attention to you AND then something pleasant happens to him when he responds correctly. This is called "compulsive" training. The correction is a sharp tug or jerk of the lead that is attached to the training collar. This produces an annoying sensation to the dog which he will learn to avoid in the future. The art of training is the timing of this correction so that the dog associates it with his own behavior, and not a random event. IF MORE THAN **ONE SECOND** ELAPSES between the dog's action and the trainers correction, the compulsive training degenerates into punishment and the dog does not understand why he is being subjected to discomfort.

There are two aspects of training which should be thought of as a sequence. The first is the dog's learning to respond to your command, and the second is the reinforcement of this learning. The readiness of the dog to learn what you teach will be dependent on your skills, particularly at getting and maintaining the dog's attention as well as the dog's own aptitude. There are dogs that are a 'quick study' and there are dogs who only are able to do remedial work.

Getting your dog's attention is easily accomplished by "bribery." The bribery takes the form of providing treats. Throughout the day speak your dog's name and as he begins to come to you praise him then give him a treat. This is positive reinforcement and **positive reinforcement** is **THE** most important part of your dogs education. If you have conditioned your dog as previously discussed then the "teaching process" will be fun for both you and your dog. Praise your dog every time you "catch him doing something right" and continue praising until you can supply a treat to your dog. Later in the book we refer to this as "treating" the dog. After feeding then stop praising. Do this when your dog comes when called, lies down and is quiet, sits by you instead of jumping on you etc. When you come for class next week you should be able to verbally praise your dog and make his tail wag!

Lesson Plan (motivational sequence):

The compulsive method which includes praising, treating, and other forms of positive reinforcement tempered with occasional negative reinforcement is the basis of all training. It is the most important technique in the beginning because it teaches the animal trust and happiness in responding to your orders. Positive motivation is used to counterbalance some of the negative feelings he will acquire from being corrected. Praising, if associated with food early, will have great emotional carryover later in the dog's life when done only with words or petting. Here we have taken advantage of Dr. Pavlov's methods of conditioning. Hence, our dog salivates in happy anticipation, not from a bell as in Dr. Pavlov's laboratory, but only from the reassuring tone of your voice.

Once your dog is coming upon your call for a treat then give a command without an immediate food reward. You will be able to see the happy, yet unfulfilled, anticipation as your dog waits for his treat. It is best to deny his treat in a step-by-step fashion rather than abruptly discontinuing it or being reconciled to carrying a bag of treats with you forever.

This step-by-step withdrawal must be carefully planned. The dog is initially praised as he approaches with the food being offered as bait. It is dangled and made visible as a teasing morsel. As the process continues the food is sporadically withdrawn from sight. This is best accomplished by holding the food behind ones back and then progressively increasing the time between the dog's arrival and your presentation of his treat. During the time that the dog is waiting for his treat you must continuously praise him in a manner identical to that used when you immediately provided his treat. The end point of this withdrawal program will be when the dog occasionally does not receive his treat at all, and you go off with him to do something else that is fun such as chasing a ball. One should not be in a hurry to withdraw food, from the dog and we have found that this process should occur over weeks rather than days. A "booster shot" treat is always valuable in energizing a dog that has become bored during your later and more advanced training.

Pay Attention

To reiterate—before we start training a dog, we must first have his attention! To accomplish this you pick up the end of the leash that your dog has been dragging around for a day or so, and walk with it in a non-restraining manner. When the dog is looking away, you say the dog's name then jerk the leash. The dog will respond by turning to look at you. This should be done several times until the dog watches his trainer. Each time that the dog looks at you alternately praise him with your voice and treat as soon as you are close enough to do so. This exercise MUST be done on a loose lead. The mistake most commonly made is tugging or pulling the dog thus depriving him of his own motivation to come to you. You are making the decision by physically pulling the dog, rather than permitting the training process to cause the dog to come to you out of his volition. Our anxiety to get

153

INDUCIVE TRAINING

the dog to come must be restrained (patience) as we realize that pulling and tugging will only inhibit and prevent the training result we seek.

Remember that in the beginning the training collar and leash should be left on your dog any time he is with you—at home, in the car, etc. This "attention getting" exercise should become a way of life for your dog. Continue this exercise until your dog will not venture away from you. Your dog will become your shadow. Correct timing, consistency, and motivating are essential. If your dog is always well supervised then your training will be one hundred percent consistent. Your dog will learn quickly. Remember: **NEVER LEAVE THE TRAINING COLLAR ON YOUR DOG WHEN HE IS UNSUPERVISED,** but **ALWAYS** have the collar on when he is within your supervision.

After your dog responds to his name by either looking at you when on lead or coming to you when off lead, the reinforcement aspect of dog training begins. Keep treats with you, carry them on your person or in a small bowl. Great food stuffs may be found anywhere in your home when the dog does the "right" thing. Once your dog is responding correctly in the house then extend his training to the outdoors.

Any dog worth his salt will try to get a treat without working for it. This process is called "stealing." Just as with people, stealing is against the rules. An easy way of preventing this is by "setting a trap." The opened treat container can be available to the dog but positioned closely to you. We have found that while watching television the available treat container is often targeted by the dog who usually has much less interest in what is on the TV screen than you do. Acting as if you are not paying attention you can "burst" into action startling the dog when he is caught pilfering. The action can be a harsh word, a jerk on his lead, or a shake by the scruff of his neck. It is a good idea several moments later to give the dog a command from which you can rightfully reward him from the container. This repeated contrast between reward and theft provides a good deterrence to potential problems such as stealing food from the table.

"Sit"

There are several commands which are essential for canine manners so that you have a safe, courteous protector in your home. Your dog's reaction to your command must be immediate or even reflexive. Speedy response denotes reliability. A protective dog will frighten many people who are invited into your home. Demonstration of your absolute control usually will calm their fears and apprehension. A

LEARNING TO SIT FOR A TREAT.

properly administered "sit" command can immediately provide relief to a visitor who is being sniffed or investigated by your protector.

The sit command can be taught easily to a young puppy using food. Command the dog, "Sit," as you present a treat held over and slightly behind your puppy's head. Repeat, "Sit" over and over as the treat gets closer. Your pup will respond in one of two ways. He will submit or become aggressive. If he submits he will sit, in which case you instantly give him the treat. This sudden sitting is obviously not because he immediately understands the word "sit" but rather it is a submissive and begging posture that the dog performs out of frustration. The other response is not the submissive sitting but the dog leaps at the treat in an attempt to snatch it even though it is held out of reach. Avoid quickly pulling the treat from the puppy's reach. This will only encourage the active response. It is best to actually push your hand containing the treat toward the active puppy. If this doesn't work then step on the leash so as to shorten its length and prevent a successful jump. We have found that a puppy so restrained also will eventually assume this sitting position.

In another chapter we describe the sitting exercise as an example of how communication can be established between trainer and dog. In this example our primary motivation is negative. In short this system describes initially pressing the rear section of the dog while simultaneously jerking up on the lead as the command "sit" is spoken. This will certainly teach a dog to sit, but with an inexperienced trainer the enthusiasm and confidence we seek in future protective animals can be diminished when using this technique. It is interesting that the dog who does not enjoy training and responds slowly to commands reacts this way as a result of inconsistent training rather than from the administration of compulsive methods.

As your dog "gets the idea," training becomes fun. See how fast you can make your dog sit, four times in a row. You command, "Sit," your dog sits, you praise and feed, then command free and start over with the sit command. We call this four time repeating of an exercise an "interval." Your training session should last two or three minutes containing two or three sit-feed-free intervals. Soon your dog will become very enthusiastic every time you begin an interval. Training is fun! You should arrange to spend four sessions with your dog daily, containing four intervals each.

How To Teach "Down"

Having your dog suddenly lie down on command can prevent a disaster. If your dog is in "hot pursuit" the motivation is exceedingly strong, such as greeting a friend who dropped by unannounced. The down command must be well enough reinforced to overcome his hunting or pursuit drive. Begin training the down at the youngest possible age.

Hold a treat on the floor in your right hand and push down on the dogs shoulder blades with your left, saying, "Down," as you do. As soon as the dog's elbows reach the ground then praise and open your hand and allow the food to be eaten. If the dog attempts to raise up then repeat, "Down," and again push down on his shoulder, but don't feed him this time. When he is calmly downed then command, "Free," and play enthusiastically with your dog. Now do an interval of four downs.

In this instance, our dog's motivation has been established by using a treat and he has learned what to do by our pushing him into the proper position. In contrast to the sit exercise, the dog does not have a natural down response and requires our prodding. To insure the dog's understanding of this command we have developed reinforcement exercises called "proofing" in which we pull upward on the leash while the dog is in the down position. We seem to contradict ourselves by commanding, "Down," as we pull upward on the lead. If the dog responds by answering to our tug rather than to our command, "Down," then he is corrected by a sharp jerk on his collar. In this way he actually learns to fight and resist being pulled out of the down position when the command has been given. This down command cannot be overtrained or over reinforced. It is often the command of last resort as we try to stop a dog from doing something that he shouldn't do. It may even involve saving him from something that could hurt him or others.

The down command must then be executed even when we are not in the dogs "line of sight." Position yourself so that your dog cannot see you, (your dog must be dragging a leash or a long line) yet you are able to see his response. Peek around a tree or other object and command, "Down." If he responds, run to him, praise him vocally and deliver a treat. The command down even when you cannot be seen should generate anticipation of a treat. If your dog does not respond to the down command you immediately appear and speak to him harshly as you approach and jerk him into the down position. In this way your presence or absence with the command is not important, as he will expect a reward if he responds and a correction if he does not.

The down command can be used to maintain the dog in a single place for long periods of time. We have kept dogs in this position (the down stay) for hours at a time. This is accomplished by placing the dog in a down position and then leave his line of sight. As in the instance before, if your dog gets out of this position you should reappear speaking harshly, "No," and correcting. If he remains down, you will appear after some interval and reward him with a treat.

This exercise can only be done when your dog reflexively downs at your command whether you are in his line of sight or not.

In contrast to the motivational technique we have described above the classic method of teaching the down is as follows:

1. Begin with your dog in the basic position (sitting at your left side).

2. Hold the lead firmly in both hands at about the level of your belt buckle. Allow enough slack in the leash, between your grip and the dog's collar, to reach knee level.

3. Command, "DOWN." Place your left foot over the lead and transfer your weight from your right foot to your left. When your left foot reaches the ground the dog should be down. If the dog has not gone down, then lift your left foot slightly and pull more lead through (your foot will become closer to the leash snap or dog's collar). Once again lower your left foot and command, "Down." Continue until the dog is down.

4. THE MOST DAMAGING TRAINER ERROR is when your dog resists and you give up. Now the dog is learning to be the trainer, he is training you! He is discovering that if he fights he can avoid correction, an extremely bad lesson for the dog. NO MATTER WHAT HAPPENS ALWAYS WIN, ALWAYS END UP WITH YOUR DOG IN THE DOWN POSITION.

These methods of compulsively teaching the dog's name (paying attention), the sit command, and the down command, illustrate how training methods can effect the character development of your dog. Understanding limits and controls are imperative for the safe, effective home protector.

Creating submission in your pet by abusive, heavy-handed correction and lack of praise will defeat your purpose to build a safe, bal-

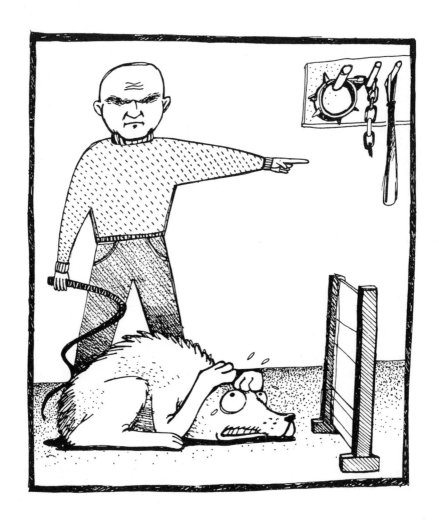

TO TRAIN IS **NOT** TO PUNISH...AN ANGRY TRAINER IS AN ABUSIVE TRAINER...COMPULSIVE TRAINING IS **NOT** TORTURE.

anced protective dog. The strong, clear headed protective dog is a happy confident animal that looks to the handler for direction. It is not a slumped-over, tail-between-the-legs, beaten down animal.

Punishment is defined by professional trainers as negative stimulus applied without reason—hurting a dog for no reason— correction that is too late. Punishment frequently results from anger. It has no place in compulsive training.

Successful training requires the trainer to understand the difference between punishment and correction. A negative stimulus to a dog such as a collar jerk will not diminish his confidence if it takes place immediately after the dog's faulty action. We call this timing. The time span between action and correction must be short enough that the dog perceives the "reason" for the correction—never more than one second! A puppy can avoid future correction by not repeating the same action.

Dogs do not understand nor do they seek revenge. A dog that is punished will not get back at his handler next week. A dog that is punished will try to save his life through aggression or submission.

Other forms of punishment are usually the result of our own human weaknesses. We become angry and over-correct. We violently jerk the leash several times to teach a puppy to sit. Instead of learning the puppy seeks only to defend himself from this torture. The puppy will typically strike out and attempt to defend himself or he will submit.

If the puppy strikes out to defend himself the trainer usually will increase the intensity of his correction and physically dominate the dog. Continued abuse will ultimately cause the puppy to go limp, play dead and submit. This will destroy the dog's confidence to challenge anyone at anytime. The dog is being taught to accept abuse passively as a means to make it stop. Common sense dictates that this dog will become worthless as a challenge to a stranger.

Another response by the trainer would be to stop the abusive corrections in response to the dog's aggressive display. This is equally bad as the dog is being taught that he can defy commands through aggression. One does not need a crystal ball to see where this will lead.

Schutzhund Giant Schnauzer pulls sled for children.

Safety

Protection of the dog's health and keeping him free from injury is our most basic responsibility to the dog. This concern is highest with the young puppy and as the animal matures the safety of those around him becomes increasingly more important. As the puppy grows older the concern for safety is for the people in the dog's life. Some things as simple as a canine greeting—jumping up—can result in serious injury to an elderly person. Adults as well as children can be injured by dogs by bumping, tripping over them, as well as being bitten. For one who intends to have a protective dog, either large or potentially aggressive, the consideration of safety must be a top priority.

The worst-case scenario that can happen to a dog owner is if his pet maims or kills a human being. One hundred-fifty-seven dog bite related deaths were recorded from 1976 to 1987 in the United States. It is an unfortunate fact that because of their size, innocence, and desire to cuddle furry animals, children under ten are the most frequently and the most seriously injured victims of canine attack. A review of the dogs involved in serious dog bite cases yields a surprising variety of culprits. Dogs classified as pit bulls were responsible for forty two percent of all fatalities and their percent is rising. German Shepherd dogs are the next most serious and frequent offenders. This number, however, should be statistically understood. German Shepherds are one of the most popular breeds and therefore their total numbers may be related to the relative frequency of dog bite cases in which they are involved.

Due to their reputation as good guard dogs German Shepherds also have been exploited by indiscriminate breeders with little understanding of the optimal protective temperament. This now is also occurring with the Rottweiler. These breeders have been responsible for developing unstable, fearful, and potentially dangerous animals that they have advertised as being "protective." This problem is often worsened, when these shy-sharp dogs are left untrained and unattended. The final result is an accident waiting to happen—an accident that too often occurs when these animals are exposed to children. The majority of deaths in children have been the result of "pet" dogs. These dogs are a dreadful threat to any family. No child is safe with a dog which is a product of unstable breeding and has been purposely isolated or ignored in his formative months. Children under two years of age are the most common fatal victims of dog attacks.

YOU CANNOT GUARANTEE CANINE SAFETY BY BUYING A "SAFE" BREED. It has been shown that, proportionately, other breeds such as Malamute, Husky, and small dogs such as the Cocker Spaniel have injured children and killed infants. Recently there have been a number of new entrants into the rogues gallery of canine muggers. These include two breeds whose popularity is increasing—the Rottweiler, and the American Pit Bull Terrier and its related type, American Staffordshire Terrier. The latter types include the famed pit-dog fighter of illegal dog sports. One must realize that although we tend to stereotype the breed most likely to injure a child, any breed, including Pekingese, can inflict injury on an infant, toddler, or confident adolescent.

What then can one do to protect children? Certainly if you are bringing a biting-protective dog into the house as an adult animal he cannot be treated as a pet by the children of the home. We think this condition should be totally avoided and only the most extreme circumstances would warrant creating a situation that could provoke a tragic accident. The majority of dog-related fatalities in the United States are not from police/guard dogs (2.8%) but from pets (64%).

In contrast to an adult dog introduced into a household where he must be physically separated from children when not in the direct supervision of an adult, a protective dog raised as a puppy can easily be programmed to accommodate children. Children's interaction with a young dog builds confidence in the animal and introduces him to the ups and downs of children's moods. Members of the household can supervise children's play with the dog and guide the children's education along with the developing protective dog. It is important that children understand the mutual respect that they have developed with the dog is not automatically transferred to their friends. The affection the dog shows them, and their desire to hug him and touch him, extends ONLY to them. Also they cannot expect that strange dogs will behave in the same way as their dog. Unfortunately serious injuries have occurred when children raised in homes with dogs have approached a seemingly friendly strange dog in the same manner they do

164

their own. These are usually dogs confined in a yard or chained. It is ironic that children who have been exposed to their own animal are often more at risk than the fearful or even phobic child who shrinks from or screams hysterically at the approach of a dog.

The general principles of safety discussed with regard to children are easily extended to adults. Two million people are bitten by dogs each year in the U.S. Since an adult will have primary responsibility for maintenance of the dog while he is in training, it is important that he know the early warning signs that denote trouble ahead in his household. The most common source for injury is the handler-aggressive dog. This type of behavior found in certain aggressive dogs is ABSOLUTELY unacceptable. It occurs when the dog is denied what he wants and responds with aggression to his owner. The dog is in this instance trying to train the owner. In his natural state the canine seeks dominance through threat and force. It is important that attempt at dominance (leadership) is recognized in its early stages. It will progress and become worse if not immediately curtailed.

Growling, or snapping gestures at the owner are cardinal sins! If one recognizes this problem in an adult dog, he should not try to stop it by himself but seek professional help. The reason for this is that ending aggression towards the owner by the dog often requires a test of wills in which the human must accomplish dominance over the dog. This type of contest, with a dog bred and trained for aggressive behavior, can lead to unwanted results and/or serious injury. It should also be realized that if the dog is challenged and the dog "wins" his resolve to dominate will be strengthened and he will persist in seeking to gain his way by threat or force.

If a guard dog is purchased, the new owner must learn the rules of safety. A trained protective dog brought into your home should not be regarded as a friend, relative, pet, or fraternity brother. He should be looked upon more as an employee and your home as his present place of employment. In this context mutual respect is clearly required. Additionally, during the initial weeks of his introduction into your home you should seek advice from the party who sold him to you. Specifically, you should be told where to house the animal, how to define his territory, and most importantly when he is loose, how problems can be avoided. Mishaps almost always involve unsuspecting individuals trespassing through the territory of this dog. Unbolted garden gates, or unlocked doors can make the mailman, the meter-man, and your friend or neighbor dropping in unannounced, fair game for your new bodyguard. Obviously possession of this animal can be both dangerous and awkward. It certainly does not fit into the carefree life style that so many Americans take for granted. A guard dog is not an accepted member of the "Pepsi Generation!"

As owners of a guard dog which is "the real thing" we must, at all cost, avoid being a SHOWOFF. We recall such an owner who was roughhousing with her boyfriend under the watchful eye of her canine protector. To be funny she commanded her dog to "bite." He promptly did so, with great enthusiasm. Her jest with the dog put her boyfriend in the hospital for a painful and expensive stay! The opportunity for the protective dog to perform his job in a real life situation may never occur. Curiosity can lead the owner into creating a staged test of the dog. This mini-drama, often employing friends as actors, can end in serious injury when the dog responds (as he has been trained to do) to threat or intrusion. Despite the fact there was no intention to do harm, ignorance and carelessness caused the "accident." Thinking that the dog is controlled through training or being physically restrained by a leash or chain can lead to disaster. Avoid any 'dress rehearsal' with an unsuspecting jogger, or salesman at your front door. These volunteer actors will be taken seriously by your dog.

Safety for the owner of the protective dog also extends to his own conduct with regard to other people's dogs. It is common for the first-time dog owner, protective or otherwise, to become an 'expert' after a few months. It is much like the neophyte sports car drivers so well known to insurance companies. They have accidents only after the initial anxiety of their unfamiliarity with sports car driving wears off. After having obtained a trained dog or having brought a dog through initial levels of protective training, one's confidence can exceed one's ability. As an example we have seen individuals attempt to train someone else's dog in similar fashion and then witnessed their embarrassment in the emergency room as they try to explain why their friend's Boxer bit them as they "tested it for aggressive instincts."

There can be no all-encompassing rule book for canine safety. The development of a **safe attitude** is mandatory. A safe attitude entails humility on the part of the trainer and his having respect for the dog and his capabilities. A safe attitude precludes using the dog as your alter ego. It requires that you place physical barriers between children

166

and the dog and that you educate children to understand the uniqueness of each animal. A safe attitude does not presume to place the dog in a position to require judgement as to which person is good and which is bad. A safe attitude is one that presumes the worst and takes the necessary steps to avoid it. Untrained dogs in the presence of unsupervised children create a dangerous and volatile mixture.

OUT OF CONTROL

SCHUTZHUND TEST

Schutzhund: A Protection Dog Sport

During late nineteenth and early twentieth centuries European dog breeders were rapidly developing the modern breeds of working dogs. These included the German Shepherd, Doberman Pinscher, Giant Schnauzer, and Bouvier Des Flandres. The animals were bred for herding, protection, and obedience qualities. A founder of the German Shepherd breed, Max vom Stephanitz, was passionately seeking to standardize the optimal utility temperament in his new breed. To test the qualities of their dogs breeders would hold local sporting contests and it was from these informal competitions that the sport of Schutzhund began.

This dog sport slowly found a following in the United States in the late 1960s. In the United States there was no tradition of protection-oriented competitive dog sports. The sport tests each dog through various levels of achievement in obedience, tracking and protection work—dog against an aggressor in defense of his handler. The act of testing a dog's ability to act forcefully in this manner was then, and still remains to some, a controversial issue.

The new Schutzhunder often finds standard obedience competition with his dog a bit tame. Intrinsic to the sport of Schutzhund is a test of the dog that exposes his character in such a way that the results are difficult to excuse or misinterpret. A dog who runs from the aggressor automatically fails the examination, as does the dog who shows fear at the sound of a gun shot (a blank of course). What you see in Schutzhund is what the dog is made of and trained to be—for better or worse. We will find out if we own Rin Tin Tin or Benji. Questions of whether the dog will climb obstacles, jump buildings in a single bound are answered. We will test his ability to follow the exact path a man walked an hour earlier and locate the wallet that he dropped in deep grass. We will find out if the dog can and will protect us.

These challenges (not leaping over tall buildings) are part of the testing process that has been incorporated into the sport of Schutzhund. After we have chosen our puppy, raised him to the best of our ability, and started his training we attempt this European sporting

Rare Neapolitan Mastiff, "Lulu Di Alaric," is clearly the "right stuff."

challenge which has so altered our concept of what the ideal protection temperament in our dogs should be.

"Schutzhund" means protection dog in German. It is an extremely demanding sport both for the dog and the trainer. Its great value is in testing the temperament, athletic ability, and protective instincts of the dog and the patience, common sense, and rapport that the trainer has with his animal.

Sometimes just roughhousing will build confidence and heighten drive to win.

This sport is vastly different from any other competitive sport seen in the American dog world. In this sport, the dog **bites!** It is this aspect of the sport which generates the greatest controversy and provokes rabid comments by those who oppose it. Understanding Schutzhund is to understand the dog. Schutzhund assumes the utility-type breeds WILL bite and assigns penalties for lack of control. To excel in this sport the dog must have courage to bite in several threatening situations and be under absolute control of his handler at all times. The owner of any large dog must recognize the natural instincts of the dog to protect and bite when appropriate. If biting is objectionable to the owner of a large utility-type animal then that person must learn to control the dog's natural inclination to be protective or buy a smaller and potentially less dangerous breed. A fundamental aspect of the working/protective types is his steadiness, instinct for protection of territory, and defense of home and hearth.

In a very controlled sequence this competition evaluates separate abilities of the animal. They are: Obedience, Tracking, and Protection. The most popular breed used in this sport is the German Shepherd. The American Kennel Club obedience routines were originated and promoted by a Poodle breeder. The exercises in the sport of Schutzhund were developed by the German Shepherd breeders in Germany. These exercises were created to explore and challenge the trainability, character, and physical attributes of the German Shepherd as a working dog. In this context, 'working' means the dog's ability to serve man—primarily as a police, security, or protection dog. German Shepherd breeders are successful in the improvement of their breed by employing Schutzhund's very demanding selection process. In Germany it became mandatory that only the competitor who had established his competence and ability on the Schutzhund field would be permitted to breed. Fearful, unstable, untrainable, or physically defective dogs were effectively weeded out of the breeding programs. The success of this method encouraged fanciers of other utility breeds to enter their dogs in Schutzhund competitions. Presently the sport of Schutzhund actively engages the Rottweiler, Bouvier des Flanders, Doberman Pinscher, Boxer, Airedale Terrier, American Staffordshire Terrier, Belgian Malinois, and Giant Schnauzer. Exceptional dogs of all of these breeds are highly prized. They contribute significantly to the likelihood that excellent quality in their litters will make them prime candidates for future home protectors.

The fundamental aspect of this sport for the future puppy purchaser is the effect it has on the selection of breeding stock. Schutzhund titles of the sire and dam make the litter far more valuable. What is the reason for this emphasis upon temperament evaluation as proven in competition? It is a way of enhancing the likelihood that the purchase of dogs from these lines will be trainable, athletically capable, protective, and reliable—for these are the traits that the Schutzhund sport examines and values.

Just as there are verifiable ways to screen congenital physical deformities—such as hip dysplasia by x-ray, genetic disease (such as Von Wilebrands disease) by blood test, and lack of conformity to a breed standard by show ring exhibition—so may temperament be evaluated.

In the United States temperament evaluation is performed only to a limited degree. In addition to the Schutzhund sport the American Temperament Testing Society (ATTS) has been one of the few other organizations seeking to test, evaluate, and record temperament. Unfortunately the total number of dogs evaluated in comparison to the number available for purchase remains woefully small.

What has this lack of temperament evaluation wrought? This is a broad and complex subject but you will find that few knowledgeable breeders would suggest that temperament evaluation has improved the quality of dogs in the United States. For protective-type breeds, there is often an unconscious attempt to soften the dog so as to make him more marketable to the general public. This not a criticism, but rather a recognition that there are cultural forces at work in breeding dogs. Thus, we have often developed two breeds with the same name. The German Shepherd of Europe is both physically and mentally a very different dog from the breed carrying the same name in the United States. The European dog is bred for his ability to jump, accept strict obedience, not flinch at sudden noises (even gunfire), and be willing to protect his master. In the United States breeding for other qualities—particularly the physical characteristics desired in "show dogs"—has dramatically reduced the other qualities maintained in his European cousin. Appreciation of these facts has become a growing force in the U.S. and is largely responsible for both the development of the Schutzhund sport here and the incorporation of Schutzhund tests by the German Shepherd Club in their Working Dog Trials.

What is the difference between a Schutzhund dog and what is commonly called an 'attack dog' or 'guard dog?' We tend to think of a

Schutzhund dog as a trained athlete whose prowess, skill, intellect, and coordination have been rigorously examined and proven in the heat of competition. He is like the professional baseball player, boxer, or track star. He is quite different from a bouncer, mugger, or bar room bully. The Schutzhund is a sport dog that participates in a stylized form of combat. Utilizing different training techniques, he could be re-channeled to more serious endeavors.

The greatest benefit in the sport of Schutzhund is the training it imparts to the dog's owner. Starting with an eight to twelve week old puppy the owner learns to discipline and correct without creating submission and fear in the dog. Training a happy confident dog is the essence of the sport.

Aggressive ability flows from the dog's confidence, not his fear. Stability of behavior and tolerance of sudden change in his environment, whether sight or sound, is fundamental to the Schutzhund dog. Clearly the benefit with regard to children is obvious. To the uninformed observer it is a mystery how this Schutzhund dog, trained to attack, is a safe, predictable family companion. The well-trained Schutzhund dog graciously tolerates the games of children. It is the untrained, fearful, often spoiled dog that bites a child.

Schutzhund training best started with puppies. An adult begins with "prey" training just like a puppy.

END OF THE TRAIL

Protection Training—The Real Thing

The ultimate form of protection that can be provided by a dog is in his attacking a human. When this happens the dog is behaving in an unnatural way.

As a predator a dog will kill small animals or the young of larger animals that cannot defend themselves. The kill of a large animal is accomplished by a joint pack effort. In this way dogs or wolves minimize injury to any single pack member. The natural instinct of any canine is to not attack a member of a larger species by himself. When we train a dog to attack a man we are developing an unnatural behavior. The unnatural behavior of biting, attacking, and closing with a man requires psychological alteration of the "natural dog."
The degree of training that is necessary can best be understood when one recognizes that the most ferocious wild canine—the wolf—has never attacked a man even when hungry and in pack strength.

In this book, we have attempted to show how the development of confidence is mandatory in the growth and training of a full-fledged protection dog. This confidence means the dog must have experienced extreme familiarity with people, and permits the dog to feel that he cannot be injured or defeated by a man. The 'protection dog' must be at ease among men and have been thoroughly trained to repress his normal retreat and escape reflexes when confronted with a threat.

This conditioning begins with the young puppy roughhousing with his trainer. The art of the training is to stimulate the puppy even when he experiences some degree of discomfort. The dog learns not to fear injury, and that he can be touched, shaken, lifted off his feet, and tugged at without harm. He is learning that human touch is not dangerous. As the dog becomes older, larger, and stronger the intensity of the roughhousing should increase.

The dog's response to roughhousing will be to assert himself. As the wild canine will do, he will nip, seize our clothing, and challenge us for possession of an object. The difference between the dog and the wild canine is that the dog learns to be assertive and even dominant to large animals NOT WITHIN HIS SPECIES. One reason that domesticated dogs that have become feral (wild) are so dangerous is that they have no inhibition or fear of man. It is the same result that happens with "garbage dump bears," who are conditioned to seeing people and getting close to them without danger to themselves. Unlike a wild (unconditioned) bear they will enter a man's territory—his car, his tent, his cabin—and drive him away from anything they think is edible. The man is of no consequence to them, just as he is of no consequence or threat to a highly-conditioned attack dog.

It is clear then that the attack dog must be a confident animal, disdainful of anyone's ability to hurt him. Since he does not fear men, he looks forward to vanquishing them when commanded by his trainer. The most important difference between this dog and the 'junk yard dog' is apparent. The junk yard dog is not confident—he is an insecure, scared, cornered animal. His territory is an enclosed area and he is fearful of strangers intruding into his space. The dog's fear generates defensive reaction at the sight of a stranger. He is not comfortable with human beings and reacts like a cornered wild animal. He rushes the fence to drive an intruder away just as a wild animal with his escape route blocked will act defensively. Unlike the heavily socialized attack dog, this animal would flee and not fight given the choice. The junk yard dog is a totally unsuitable type to be kept in the home because he can "go off" at whatever he perceives as a threat—the opposite of the trained and controlled, confident attack dog.

To train a dog to become a 'protection dog' requires professional help. Those who choose to raise an attack animal should carefully review our significant concerns regarding this process. To continue the training you should expect to follow the type of program described below.

Beginning with a mature dog, usually eighteen months or older, your trainer will test him to decide if he is suitable for your requirements. The dog must be tied on a short lead in an unfamiliar place—preferably indoors. He will test in three major areas.

First—To exclude a dog that doesn't have the starch to protect himself, the trainer will approach the dog. Since this is not a junk yard dog he must be confident, not shy away and not display aggressive response to the trainer's neutral behavior.

Second—This "sound" animal will now have a more intense confrontation with the trainer. While tied by a short chain or cable, without his owner present, the professional protection trainer or

176

agitator will threaten the dog while he approaches him. This threat will be manifested by his posture as he slowly advances on the dog while maintaining eye contact and projecting an aggressive image.

The ideal dog will become uneasy but not submissive. This is an important distinction because some dogs have learned to get along in their human pack by slinking, currying favors, or rolling over. These actions, often believed cute by the family, are simply the dog acknowledging the human's strength and dominance. Our protection-dog-candidate does not do these things with a stranger. He may be confused at first since this is a novel situation. But he will stare back, not shift his gaze, and challenge the approaching stranger. The aggressive dog will display his own size to the agitator by standing erect, almost puffing himself up to a more imposing appearance. At this point the agitator has established that this dog, with training, can be made to behave aggressively. It is an error for the trainer to continue beyond this level of confrontation during an introductory session. The dog does not know what he can do beyond this degree of holding his ground.

Third—The final test requires the owner to return to the side of his dog. Now the dog is a member of a pack again. It is only a two member pack, but this is a very important difference to a social animal like the dog. In contrast to the domesticated house cat's behavior, the dog is influenced by his sense of support and mutual dependence with his other pack member, the owner. The third test is done with the dog and owner cornered together. The agitator approaches the pair with suspicious and provocative gestures. The dog is much more likely to be confident and may challenge the agitator more aggressively. Besides eye contact, the dog should bark or lunge. These are the responses that the agitator will build on in future training.

Civil agitation is a form of training that teaches the dog to behave aggressively. This training instills distrust of a man in a dog that was formerly perfectly comfortable with people. The dog learns that not everyone is his friend. Since he has no fear of people the agitator provokes the dog to dominate and drive him off. A fearful dog (junk yard) might also demonstrate an aggressive display but with the significant difference that the fearful dog will flee if given the chance.

The basis of civil agitation revolves around isolation of the dog. Basic training is started by isolating the dog. Alone, the animal is without the reassurance of his pack. For the domestic dog his pack is his owner. The dog is challenged by the agitator in the same manner as

Why Doberman Pinschers can intimidate is obvious.

in the second examination. The agitator then approaches the dog and threatens him. The body language of the agitator signals that this is a hostile approach by a stranger. From our testing we can expect the dog to hold his ground, growl and bark. This counter aggression by the dog will cause the agitator to run away confirming, in the dog's mind, that the human is timid and afraid. By continuing this training over several weeks the agitator will increase this aggressive conditioning by constantly withdrawing from the dog. This challenge by the agitator and the dog's perception that the challenger is unable to harm the dog continues to increase the animals confidence and security. Eventually the agitator will reach a point so close to the dog that the dog may snap and clearly indicate that he wants to bite. The dog is doing this because his previously learned response of barking has now proved inadequate.

For legal and safety purposes most people should not have their dogs taken beyond this point. A dog displaying ferocious aggression is a highly intimidating sight even without 'the bite.' In nearly all circumstances in our society this display will suffice as a satisfactory deterrent. The dog trained in civil agitation cannot be frightened back from his aggression by anything an agitator or intruder can do. The dog has been conditioned to make a savage display until the agitator withdraws. In a real life situation, an intruder facing a large aggressive animal restrained by his owner would have to be in an irrational state to push any further. It can be expected that the intruder will attempt to flee. Instead of running away the intruder may present a threat to the dog and the dog will meet this threat with an even more violent response.

A competent trainer recognizes that civil agitation requires actual "street" training to be of value. Training for real live "street situations" must be varied by place and person. Different agitators will challenge the dog. They will do this by surprising the dog in many situations. Without this combat technique, the dog may learn only a stereotyped defense response. Our dog is primed to behave defensively in ANY situation. We avoid the mistake of training only at the training school.

Complete civil agitation should include creating situations that might actually occur in the owner's environment. These include both daytime and night confrontations, in the owners home, as he exits his car, walking alone, and in more crowded situations such as a parking

SOUND ALERT

German Shepherd Dog. Classic common breed working dog.

lot. Confrontations also include agitators of various physical appearances including those of different size, race and gender. Also both vocal and silent agitators are useful.

It is even more effective to associate a trigger command word that will cause the dog to bark in an aggressive way even before he clearly identifies the threat. The owner, with his superior intellect, can identify a potential danger before the dog can discern it. The dog's hearing and sense of smell is much more acute than man's. Yet the subtlety of human behavior that might pose a danger may be apparent to a man before the dog is alerted. Therefore the owner may be called upon to arouse the dog to a defensive posture before the dog determines that they are in jeopardy.

An aspect of civil agitation that can be used to accelerate the dog's aggressive behavior is to agitate him while he is surrounded by other dogs. These other dogs have already learned the threat-and-counter threat game. When the agitator approaches the novice dog and he is tied two feet from a dog on either side of him, he is under tremendous pressure to join in. Your dog learns from other dogs more quickly than he would alone. The strong pack behavior is being aroused. Doing this multiple dog agitation allows us to use the animal's pack instincts for defense of his territory.

Training has thus far stopped short of allowing the dog to bite a human. Bite development is understood as a natural extension of the confidence and aggressive response techniques that have been used to get the dog to bark violently. To move the dog into biting is accomplished by the agitator providing an opportunity. Until this point the agitator has kept his body and arms short of the lunging dog's muzzle. He has progressively gotten closer to the dog with each training session, and the dog has become so intense that he is now at a level of frenzied aggression. There is no relief for the dog at this stage of training. He cannot reach the man and he cannot drive him away. This frustration frees the dog from his inhibitions. He now has only one consuming drive—attack the man. Suddenly the agitator brings his arm, covered with a protective sleeve, within striking distance and you can bet your hat it will be seized by the dog. The agitator sheds the sleeve immediately and flees. The animal's aggression is vented by violently ripping the arm from the agitator. In one clear moment the dog has learned that he can bite a man! He can hurt a man, make him run away and nothing has happened to him. It is at this moment that the transition is made to "the real thing"—an **ATTACK DOG!**

All training after this will serve the purpose of increasing intensity of the attack and teaching the dog the tactics of the game.

The beginnings of this game was taught by our early conditioning entertainments with the young puppy. The tug of war games, though they might have included growling, were always a game to the dog. It was a game because the dog always won, and more importantly, he was never injured or forced to back down. These games were always comfortable and fun because they were with his owner, who had earned the puppy's trust. The puppy never learned fear, submission, or the sense that he was fighting for his life. The seeds of confidence from puppy games have flowered in our attack dog. Even as he grabs the sleeve from the agitator he is not doing so in fear, and he is not fighting for his life. He is excited, frustrated, and aggressively trying to seize the man. It is a game that has been taught, and it is not a game known by wild animals. The dog is not behaving like a tiger seizing its prey—he is not killing to eat. He is not defending his young. He is acting from the way he was conditioned beginning when he was only eight weeks old. He is dominating and controlling a human as he has done many, many times.

The bite-work has been a conditioned development. It can be extended far beyond the point an untrained animal would ever attempt. A dog can be conditioned to attack and continue his assault until the man is dead. This is the result of training and not the natural behavior of a dog.

He can be conditioned to ignore threats and pain. This again is not the natural response of a dog. Attack work is training and conditioning. In his training the dog was never defeated and he only recognizes victory. The wielding of a stick, shovel, gun, or club by the aggressor is taught as something that can be overcome. This is accomplished by striking the dog lightly with these objects or firing blank cartridges. The intensity of the agitator's blows increase and the gun fired closer to the animal's head. The dog learns that he can fight through these defenses and think of them as merely distractions rather than obstacles.

Training teaches that the agitator can strike the dog lightly while he is firmly gripping the protection sleeve. Since puppyhood this dog has learned that even uncomfortable handling will not injure him. The agitator will increase the force in striking the animal and use hollow, soft, leather or inflatable plastic clubs that cause little pain, but generate loud contact noise. The rolled up newspaper that was used for years to discipline and terrify dogs will have no effect on our conditioned animal. Our dog knows that there is nothing the agitator can do that will defeat him. He perceives himself as invulnerable, and the harder the agitator fights the more fun the game. An unconditioned dog would panic and every second of the confrontation would require a decision for the dog whether to continue to fight or run. This is the canine's natural response—one that we have eliminated in our dog with carefully planned conditioning.

The exact mechanics of training must be learned in a supervised professional environment. None of the training techniques described here should be attempted without professional supervision. This is particularly important, as many people believe that they "know dogs." These are the people who are at the greatest risk. This level of training might be compared to sky diving. No one in his right mind would try to pack a parachute for the first time after reading a book and then jump from a plane at ten thousand feet. **NO ONE** should attempt protection training without expert guidance.

Bouvier des Flandres. Becoming more popular as protector. (Not all Bouviers are as animated as this guy.)

"Gotcha"

Theory and Practice of Training—
Realistic Expectations

The preceding chapters have described dogs, puppies, and their development as both companions and protectors. Fundamental to this development is a realistic expectation of the limitations of the canine pupil. The dog's learning ability via limited verbal understanding, requires that we treat him as something else than a slow child in a fur coat. Your properly selected puppy or dog is a motivated and willing student, who will learn by carefully administered rewards and corrections. He cannot be argued with or convinced, but rather he must be conditioned to perform what is your will. His desire to please and enthusiasm for learning tasks often exceeds that of his trainer. If these premises are true then why are there so many frustrated dog owners, disappointed dog trainers, and, in too many cases, ruined dogs?

CONFUSION is the dogs enemy and it is so often unwittingly produced over and over during his training sessions. This confusion is created by human beings projecting their feelings and interpreting the dog's momentary difficulty in mastering a task as defiance, stubbornness or stupidity. To further aggravate this problem, trainers (we use the term loosely) respond by screaming, repeating the same command over and over, and acting in a violent manner towards the dog. To those watching this from the sidelines this scene can vary from wildly humorous to downright abuse that prompts people to want to call the ASPCA.

Let us examine this human behavior from the dog's point of view. The spoken word to the dog is unintelligible gibberish. We can understand this best if we imagine suddenly being placed in a foreign country. The language would be completely incomprehensible, both as the spoken word and written material. As we drive along the road, we would do our best by following the example of other motorists, but would not be able to read the traffic signs. Suddenly, we see what appears to be a police car rapidly approaching us. We now might understand what it may be like to face an authority figure who initially assumes we understand what he is trying to communicate to us.

185

The policeman after speaking to us in a conversational tone might respond by speaking more and more loudly and slowly when we failed to react to his commands. At some point the situation could turn ugly if he was either not professional or suspected we were either defying or seeking to deceive him. The situation is even more difficult for the dog as he does not have recourse to respond in a sign language or point to some mutually understood article such as a passport.

We have witnessed innumerable owners alternately arguing, pleading, threatening, screaming, shaking their fist, leaping up and down and making the most violent gestures which if directed against another human being would provoke an instant assault or at the very least a telephone call to the nearest police station. **THIS IS NOT THE WAY TO TRAIN A DOG.**

There are many books that purport to teach you how to train a dog for a series of exercises such as sit, heel, stay, and even attack. These books would have you believe that after reading their text, and looking at the diagrams you will be able, in a facile manner, to have your dog performing these routines. We would like to describe a single exercise such as having the dog "sit" and carefully go through the necessary communication and methods of accomplishing this communication that will be required. There are no tricks or secrets, but rather an understanding of fundamentals of dog training which can be extended from basic obedience to the most advanced levels of training.

What then is correct training which can be distinguished from this "cook book" approach?

TRAINING FIRST REQUIRES COMMUNICATION. This interspecies communication between canine and human must be undertaken in a calm, relaxed, and comfortable manner. A single word must be associated with a single action. This is the most fundamental building block of training. The **art** of training is being able to accomplish this communication. A command such as "sit," as a single word has no meaning to the dog. How then can we communicate to the dog that this word indicates that he is to place his bottom on the ground ASAP. First, do not, as if addressing a human being, use the dog's proper name. This simply is verbal confusion. Only say the word "sit." The dog will need to be physically placed in the sitting posture while the word is spoken. The physical placing of the dog in a sitting position will contain a single noxious element. The dog will know that as the word is uttered a disagreeable feeling will ensue. His anticipation of this disagreeable feeling will cause him to seek to avoid it and thus as "sit" is uttered he will assume the position prior to being physically placed.

Thus the word "sit" is the verbal stimulus, placing him in a sitting position is the tactile communication, and avoidance of the disagreeable feeling (which is a "collar jerk") is its motivation.

Careful examination now permits us to understand the following sequence of training a dog to sit on your left side (heel position).

Sit and accept praise:

1) Place a training collar on the dog's neck (chain choke or pinch collar).

2) Attach a lead to the collar and grasp the lead with your right hand.

3) Clearly and calmly speak "sit" while briskly jerking the lead upward with your left hand and pressing the dog's rump downward with your right hand.

4) As soon as the dog sits let the lead go slack and praise.

This brief example demonstrates:

1) Communication, the synthesis of the verbal (not understood by the dog) "sit" with the tactile (rump being pressed down and head and neck being jerked sharply upward).

2) Motivation (Negative reinforcement) avoidance of neck being jerked and rump being pushed down.

3) Positive reinforcement—praise when done correctly, as well as relaxation from the anticipated jerk which did not occur as the dog was able to assume the correct posture before the correction was given.

Problems:

Training is an imperfect art. Our expectations of what a dog should do after being trained will always exceed reality. We become trapped by our own success as trainers. The advanced dog seems almost able to anticipate the next training step. It is at this point that some of the more serious problems arise. These problems include becoming sloppy with the original techniques we used to bring the dog to this state of readiness and trying to use short cut techniques as the dog now appears to be "learning" at a quicker rate. Worst of all, our enthusiasm for the dog's accomplishments in training make us forget the original limitations we accepted, and we then project human understanding. We regress to thinking that we can communicate verbally with our dog. This will always lead to disappointment, frustration, and finally it will be the dog that suffers.

"Does your Mother know where you are, Sonny?"

An example that springs to mind is Acki, one of the finest German Shepherds that we have seen both in structure, character and temperament in the last twenty years. This dog was imported from Germany from a knowledgeable, sincere and long acquaintance. When the dog reached us he was almost too much to behold. His bearing was regal, and after several days of becoming acquainted with our surroundings we tested him with basic protection and training routines and found that he was everything we had expected. In Germany where he had worked as a police dog, he was written up in the local newspapers after he had interrupted an attempted assault on a woman in a wooded park. While on patrol he investigated muffled screams heard behind shrubbery and quickly brought the felon into his canine custody. It was this dog that was then purchased from Germany by an American police department.

In order to assure ourselves that this rather expensive dog would satisfy the requirements of his new American trainer we had them both work together for orientation and advanced training. The police officer could not be more enthusiastic. He had never seen so much spirit, courage, and beauty in a service dog. We were filled with optimism for this police man-dog team.

Within several months of working on his new police force Acki was thrust into a serious situation. He was called out to search for and apprehend an armed felon who had escaped into a heavily wooded area. Because of the seriousness of the crime multiple police forces had converged to try to cut off points of escape from the wood. Using correct police technique Acki's trainer had the officers remain far behind him as Acki followed the trail. It was well understood by all, as night approached, that the other officers must remain far behind the dog so as to give the canine team support, yet not confuse the dogs trailing.

Into this well organized police search with an excellent dog/man team enters the variability of human behavior. A police officer who had heard the orientation sought to find the felon by himself. Using Acki and his trainer as the point team he trailed them. He had been known in the past for having made "hero" arrests and was proceeding with his independence or what might be considered a lack of regard for procedure.

As Acki closed in on the felon straining at his tracking lead a figure, gun held at arm's length stepped into the dog's field of view. In the dark his handler could not make out the figure that drew Acki's attention. Before he could swing his light to the subject he heard a shriek of pain. He raced twenty feet to where Acki wrestled in the underbrush with his assailant. His handler could make out only glimpses of the uniform in the now unconscious man. Instantly Acki released at his handlers command, Acki had made the "hero" arrest and the daredevil police officer was on his way to the hospital for surgery.

What had Acki done? He had carefully followed an hour old track through woods and failing light. Despite the sounds and the many officers behind him he kept his concentration on the trail, and suddenly recognized a threatening figure holding a gun just a few yards off the trail. As the figure moved he struck. In almost any circumstance, except the present one, he would have been saving his handlers life by his quick reaction, more acute sense and fearless behavior. The human world is much more complex, and for this reason Acki who did his job, fulfilled his training, caught an errant police officer and not the dangerous felon. This time there were no awards, newspaper articles, and commendations, but rather Acki was summarily discharged to be replaced by "a dog with more sense."

Dog training from the most basic obedience to the most demanding police work requires commitment, patience, practice, and discipline. There is no place for anger, pity, or guilt. If these emotions arise during our training we are doing something wrong. Anger originates when the dog is not doing what we want, and we project our human character upon the animal. We view it as defying us and therefore a deserving object of our displeasure—sometimes even rage. Pity arises when our corrections seem to inflict discomfort upon the dog and we empathize with him. We forget that in the natural canine pack corrections are meted out to maintain pack order by the dominant members. It is interesting that the same emotions of anger and pity are well known to those of us who have raised children and can remember our own parents telling us that "this hurts me more than it hurts you." Guilt finally arises when we reflect upon the days training, see our own mistakes, and realize that the dog simply did not understand us.

The optimal dog for us will be what we make of the puppy we receive. He will have a genetic potential if we have chosen wisely and this will include stability, enthusiasm and a sense of territory. Upon this foundation we can build our loving protector. If we obtain an older dog we will be able to more clearly know what he will be like as our companion but we also will have significantly less ability to modify him for our particular needs. In either case the loving protector is not a finished, store bought, item. Neither is he a static and unchanging object. He will grow older and show both the psychological and physical affects of maturity and aging. He will need to be retrained, shown affection, and if ignored he will deteriorate. Even at his prime, just as Acki, he will be limited to what he may be able to distinguish in the complex human world. Thus his optimal benefit will only be achieved by a trainer and friend who guides him through difficulties and understands his limitations.

There are many "how-to" dog training books but just like flying an airplane, playing a musical instrument, or learning anything that requires both physical and mental coordination, dog training cannot be learned just from books. Books can be a starting point and a future reference but only with operant learning—learning with your hands, voice and attention on the dog—will you succeed.

The rewards are immense. To reap these rewards you will have spent many long hours when your patience and persistence will have been severely tested. You will have experienced days of high accomplishment followed by days of frustration. If you entertain any doubt that you can maintain a total dedication to the goal for which you strive, you would be well advised to reassess your decision to proceed.

On the other hand, if your commitment is strong and you are excited at the prospect of your new adventure—if you have no doubt that the end result is well worth the struggle, lose no time—go find your puppy. You will have earned a friend for life, a loyal protector, and days filled with companionship and comfort.

"Magic" and buddies.